The Books of the Old and New Testaments Proved to be Canonical, and Their Verbal Inspiration Maintained and Established

THE BOOKS

OF THE

OLD AND NEW TESTAMENTS

PROVED TO BE

CANONICAL,

AND

THEIR VERBAL INSPIRATION

MAINTAINED AND ESTABLISHED;

WITH

AN ACCOUNT OF THE INTRODUCTION AND CHARACTER

OF THE

APOCRYPHA.

BY

ROBERT HALDANE, Esq.

FOURTH EDITION, ENLARGED.

EDINBURGH:

PRINTED FOR WILLIAM WHYTE & CO.
BOOKSELLERS TO HER MAJESTY;
LONGMAN & CO., J. DUNCAN, T. HAMILTON & CO.,
SEELEY & SONS, AND J. NISBET, LONDON;
AND W. CARSON, DUBLIN.

1832.

PREFACE.

The Canon and Inspiration of the Holy Scriptures are subjects of the highest importance to every Christian. The Divine Books contain the only information with respect to the salvation of sinners; and the duties, privileges, and hopes of the heirs of heaven. All that can be known of the mind of God, and of the future state of man, must be learned from them. The theories of men with respect to the things of God, and all reasonings respecting revealed subjects, grounded on any other foundation but the Divine declarations, are not only fallacious as far as concerns their immediate objects, but prevent an accurate acquaintance with the ways of God, by opening innumerable devious paths, which deceitfully promise to lead to heavenly knowledge.

The Bible not only contains things that are divinely accredited as true, but it contains all the truth on divine subjects that is accessible to man. Hence every thing that respects the particular books composing the Canon, and the inspiration of these books, is of the liveliest interest to every Christian. Whatever tends to invalidate the authority of any particular book of the Canon, or to add other books to the number, ought to be met with the most decided opposition, as threatening to rob us of the most precious revealed truth, or to impose on us the traditions of men as the commandments of God. To reject a book whose authenticity rests on the authority of the Canon, is not only to give up the portion of divine truth which such book contains, but to take away the evidence of every other book standing on the same authority. If one book of the Canon is given up, how shall any other be retained on the authority of that Canon? Is it a light matter to admit a principle that unsettles the evidence of every book of the Bible? Is it an innocent thing to charge as superfluous, unimportant, unholy, or unworthy of God, any thing that there is authority to hold as his Word? What, then, shall be said of those Christians, who have not only discovered an unbecoming facility in surrendering parts of the book of God, but have laboured with the most strenuous exertions to unsettle the Canon, and have availed themselves of every resource, with which a perverse ingenuity could supply them, to degrade some of the books that are as fully authenticated as any in that sacred collection?

In like manner, to recognise a book, not authenticated by the Canon, is to invalidate the authority of the Canon, and to lay a foundation for the admission of unaccredited books to an indefinite extent. It is obvious, that those who do so cannot be assured of the truths which they receive, nor that they have all revealed truths in the Bible. Such a mode of proceeding degrades the Word of God, unsettles the faith of the Christian, and greatly mars his edification and comfort.

The inspiration of the Scriptures is of equal importance with the authority of the Canon. If God is not the author of them, in the fullest and most complete sense of that term, we cannot receive them as the Word of God. The Scriptures so plainly assert their inspiration, that it is matter of astonishment that any who profess to believe them should have denied it. Yet many have contrived to hold the word, and to deny the thing itself. In this way, they perhaps hide even from themselves the boldness of their unhallowed speculations. That inspiration extends to words as well as to matter, is so obvious, that it never could have been questioned, if those who deny it had not misled themselves by their vain reasonings on the subject, or taken the contrary for granted without enquiry, on the authority of others. A writing inspired by God self-evidently implies in the very expression, that the words are the words of God; and the common impression of mankind coincides with this most entirely. That the inspiration is in the matter, not in the words; that one part of Scripture is written with one kind or degree of inspiration, and another part with another kind or degree, is contrary to the phraseology, and totally without foundation in any part, of the Scriptures themselves, and never could have suggested itself as a natural meaning of the word. This unholy invention is the figment of an ill-employed ingenuity, either to invalidate some Scripture truths, or to repel some objections, which appeared otherwise unanswerable. It is an expedient to serve a purpose, and as little to be approved, when it is used to defend the declarations of God, as when it is used to overturn them. Yet degrading views both of the Canon and inspiration of the Scriptures too generally prevail; and the writers of most influence on the public mind, instead of correcting these errors, lend all their influence to their establishment.

The plenary or verbal inspiration of the Holy Scriptures is not only established by the most express passages in the way of direct authority, but it is a matter of no light consideration that there are no opposing passages on the other side. ' Hardly an error ever was maintained, but what could press some passage of the Word of God into its service, by the use of torture. Indeed, very many important truths of the

Divine Word are not without their difficulties, from passages that afford a handle to human ignorance and human depravity. While these are always capable of a solution in perfect accordance with the truths to which, at first sight, they may appear to be opposed, they prove a test of our submission to the Divine wisdom. They manifest the childlike disposition of the people of God; but they are as gins and snares to the wisdom of this world, and the wise are taken by them in their own craftiness. As the contiguity of the Canaanites manifested the unbelief of the people of Israel; so these passages, in the Divine wisdom, bring out into open avowal the enmity of men to the truth of God. But the inspiration of the Scriptures in the words, as well as in the matter, is not opposed by any difficulty of this kind; and the authors of the low and derogatory view of the Word of God, which ascribes to it different degrees of inspiration, cannot plead a single passage that will afford them even the shadow of support. Their doctrine is but a theory—a theory in opposition to the most express assertions of Scripture, and not countenanced by the allegation of a single text.

Whence comes the Bible? is a question in every way worthy of the deepest attention of the Christian. The grounds on which is rested the happiness of this world, and of the world to come, can never be too deeply examined. The title-deeds to so immense an inheritance are worthy of the constant researches of the life of man.

To establish with the utmost precision what are the books belonging to the Canon of Scripture, to fix the brand of reprobation on all false pretenders to the honour of inspiration, and to vindicate the writings of the Old Testament and the New, as the words of the Spirit of God, can at no period be a useless labour. But present circumstances add greatly to this importance, and recent events have discovered not only ignorance on these subjects, where knowledge might have been expected, but opposition even from the friends of the Gospel. It is much to be regretted, that unscriptural opinions concerning these subjects have long been entertained, and have of late been advocated by persons, who might have been expected to be the most zealous in opposing their progress. The Christian public are in the greater danger from the infection of this heresy, that it is propagated by persons whom they have long been accustomed to regard as among the brightest ornaments of true religion. Had these dangerous opinions made their appearance in the works of Socinians, Christians would have stood on their guard against them. But when the Canon is unsettled, and verbal inspiration is denied by men who profess to hold the distinguishing doctrines of the Gospel, many will be misled. If, then, we are commanded to contend earnestly for the faith once delivered to the saints, it is surely our duty to contend for the Canon and Inspiration of the Bible, by which only that faith can be ascertained. Our reverence for the Bible depends on our full conviction of the plenary inspiration of the Apostles and Prophets, and our being satisfied that our Bible exclusively contains their writings. On these subjects the mind of every Christian should be fully informed and firmly established. Just views respecting them exalt our conceptions of the perfection of the Holy Scriptures, and tend to make us better acquainted with their contents. The opposite views have a contrary tendency in a very high degree.

While the natural opposition of fallen man to God leads some to open and avowed infidelity, it operates on a still greater number in the way of indifference to religion. It leads them to be satisfied with very lax and general views on a subject to which they are indisposed, but which they dare not altogether neglect. Under the influence of this indifference many entertain no fixed views in regard to the Bible. They admit that the Scriptures contain a revelation from God, and that many parts of them are, therefore, entitled to our utmost reverence; but they do not perceive that all parts of the Bible, whether history, prophecy, praise, or precepts, are so many integral and connected parts of one great whole, intimately connected with the Cross of Christ, which forms the centre of revelation, without reference to which no part can be understood. They may read the history of Israel, they may believe the facts recorded, and yet remain completely unacquainted with the instruction conveyed. They may admire the Proverbs of Solomon as the dictates of the wisest of men; they may derive benefit from them in the regulation of their conduct in the world; while their souls cleave to the dust, and they are treasuring up for themselves wrath against the day of wrath. They may read the predictions of the desolation of Tyre and Babylon; they may acknowledge the proof which these afford of the Divine foreknowledge, while they remain utterly ignorant of the nature of that kingdom to the establishment of which all such events were subservient, and with which every part of revelation is closely and inseparably connected. But when God opens the understanding to understand the Scriptures; when men are made to know that all the prophets, both in the history of the past and the predictions of the future, bear witness to Christ, and that every circumstance recorded in the Word of God, is a part of the testimony of Jesus, then they are led to exclaim, " O the depth of the riches both of the wisdom and knowledge of God;" to pray with the Psalmist, " Open thou mine eyes, that I may behold wondrous things out of thy law;" and with the Apostle, they follow on to apprehend Christ Jesus, the Lord, in the diligent study of every part of the Word of God.

This naturally produces just views on the subject of inspiration. Unless the mind be misled by false teaching, or perverted by some unscriptural theory, it puts an end to idle and impious speculations about supernatural influence being unnecessary, when the sacred penmen are speaking of " common or civil affairs ;" and about their mentioning " common occurrences or things in an incidental manner as any other plain and faithful men might do." We behold the Word of God composed of many parts, but forming one grand connected system, like a building, so admirably constructed, that every stone increases its beauty and stability, and not one of which could be removed without injury. We behold the wisdom of God in employing so many persons to labour in distant ages, and in different departments, producing in their various compositions a revelation of his will, complete in all its parts, and distinguished by the most perfect unity, without the shadow of discrepancy, redundancy, or deficiency. From not perceiving this, some attach different degrees of authority to different parts of Scripture. In the same way, many prefer the discourses of Jesus to the other portions of the New Testament, although, when about to leave the world, he informed his Apostles that there were many things which at present they could not bear, but which he would afterwards communicate to them by the teaching of his Spirit. According to his promise, he endued them with power from on high, and consequently in their writings we have the completion of divine revelation, the exhibition of the great salvation which at the first began to be spoken by the Lord, and which he more fully explained by speaking in his Apostles, 2 Cor. xiii. 3.

It is the object of the following pages to exhibit the abundant evidence by which the authenticity of the books of the Old and New Testaments is confirmed, and to prove that the inspiration to which the Scriptures lay claim, is in the fullest sense plenary in every part of them, extending both to the ideas, and to the words in which these ideas are expressed. Hence the Scripture is described as the Word of God, and the words of which it is composed are represented as proceeding out of his mouth. This language is conclusive on the subject, and by directing the sacred writers to employ it, God has ascribed to himself whatever is written in the Bible, and requires all to listen to HIS WORD with the utmost reverence. Isa. i. 2, 20.

An account is given in the following pages of the Apocryphal writings, with the reasons that forbid their being received along with the Word of God. Their usurpation of the place they have long occupied in the estimation of many, is traced to its origin; and their presumptuous claims to inspiration, or to any authority, are exploded. This is the more necessary, as many are but little acquainted with the manner in which these forgeries have obtained the situation they hold in the Bibles of Roman Catholics and even of Protestants, or with the impiety of their contents. It is proved that the Apocrypha is not a part of God's word, and that, instead of being a book of useful though uninspired instruction, it is a book of imposture and destructive delusion.

A work has just appeared from the pen of Mr Carson, in which the false theories of inspiration exhibited in some late publications, are triumphantly refuted.[*] The reader who desires to examine this important subject will find it advantageous to read that work in connexion with this publication. They both refer to it in different points of view. The one is in proof, the other in reply. The one aims

---

[*] " The Theories of Inspiration of the Rev. Daniel Wilson, Rev. Dr Pye Smith, and the Rev. Dr Dick, proved to be erroneous; with Remarks on the Christian Observer, and Eclectic Review. By Alexander Carson, A.M. minister of the gospel. Sold by W. White and Co., Edinburgh; T. Hamilton and Co., London; and W. Carson, Dublin;" &c. &c. Price 3s. 6d.

at exhibiting the evidence, and the other answers objections; and in order to have at once a view of the evidence drawn from Scripture of the doctrine of inspiration, and a solution of the most plausible cavils against it, both should be perused. A question of such importance demands full consideration, and if ingenuity has exerted its utmost efforts to shroud this subject in darkness, detail ought not to be thought tedious in restoring light and order. These publications will, it is hoped, enlarge the views and fortify the convictions of Christians respecting the Divine origin and absolute perfection of the Holy Scriptures, and will prove that those who recognise distinctions in the inspiration of the Word of God, or who make concessions that virtually subvert it, are chargeable with no slight evil. After candidly weighing what is advanced, they will have reason to conclude that in the Bible they possess the whole Word of God, and nothing but his Word. In the appendix it will be grateful to them to observe, that the views of the inspiration of the Bible maintained in these publications are not new. They will see, by a number of quotations, that, though too much neglected, and even opposed by many, the doctrine of the plenary inspiration of the Holy Scriptures has been, from the earliest times, the faith of some of the greatest ornaments of the church of God.

THE
GENUINENESS AND AUTHENTICITY
OF THE
HOLY SCRIPTURES.*

OLD TESTAMENT.

THE Bible, which contains the account of the origin, progress, and nature of the Christian religion, is the production, not of one period, but of many ages. The writers of it succeeded each other, during the space of about 1500 years. The Scriptures of the Old Testament far exceed, in antiquity, all other historical records. Moses, who wrote the five first books, lived more than 1000 years before Herodotus, the father of Grecian history; and rather earlier than the time of Herodotus, Ezra and Nehemiah completed the historical part of the Old Testament Scriptures.

The longevity of the first generations of men rendered a written revelation, between the fall of man

---

* A genuine book is one written by the person whose name it bears, as the author of it. An authentic book is one that relates matters of fact, as they really happened.

and the promulgation of the law at Sinai, less necessary, as the knowledge of the Divine will was, during that period, transmitted from one age to another, by very few individuals. From Adam to Moses, although a space of about 2500 years, it passed through only four intermediate persons. In all that time, God made himself known by visible interpositions and signs, as in the cases of Cain and Babel, and held direct communication with prophets, who were revered as such by the people among whom they lived, which tended to preserve his truth from being corrupted. Thus it was sufficiently early in the days of Moses, permanently to record that authentic revelation, which was then delivered. But, at that period, when the age of man was reduced nearly to its present limits, God separated a people from the nations, and gave them such an establishment, that full security was afforded for preserving entire his written word.

Moses, who, at the giving of the law, acted the part of a mediator between God and the people of Israel, was called up to Mount Sinai, where he received those laws and institutions that were then enjoined. These, together with the history of the creation, and of whatever, from the beginning, was necessary for the instruction of the people of God, were committed by him to writing, in five books, and deposited in the tabernacle by the side of the ark.

These five books, called the Book of the Law, and also known by the name of the Pentateuch, (or five volumes,) constitute the first part of the sacred records, and include the history of about 2550 years. The law was read every Sabbath-day in the synagogues, and again with solemnity every seventh year. The king was required to copy it, and the people were commanded to teach it to their children, and to bear it as " signs upon their hands, and frontlets between their eyes." The remaining books * of the Old Testament, composed by different writers, carry the history of Israel beyond the Babylonish captivity, and contain the messages of a succession of prophets till 420 years before the coming of Christ, when, at the distance of about 1030 years from Moses, Malachi, the last of the prophets, wrote.

The books that compose the Old Testament Scriptures, were held by the Jews, in every age, to be the genuine works of those persons to whom they are ascribed; and they have also been universally and exclusively, without any addition or exception, considered by them as written under the immediate influence of the Spirit of God. They preserved them with the greatest veneration; and, at the same time, carefully guarded against receiving any apocryphal or uninspired books. While the Jews were divided into various sects, which stood in the most direct opposition to each other, there never was any difference among them respecting the authority of the sacred writings.

The five books of Moses were also preserved by the Samaritans, who received them nearly 700 years

---

* The exact time when the book of Job was written is not known.

before the coming of Christ. Whatever disagreement, in other respects, subsisted between them and the Jews, and however violent their enmity against each other, they perfectly united in admitting the authenticity and inspiration of the law of Moses, which they both adopted as their religious rule. In addition to all this, about 280 years before the Christian era, the whole of the Old Testament was translated into Greek; a language which, from the time of Alexander's conquests, was commonly understood by the nations of the world. *Thus Jews, Samaritans, and all the civilized world, had access to these sacred books,* which prevented the possibility of their being either corrupted or altered without its being generally known.

We are assured by Josephus, the Jewish historian, who was born about five years after the death of Christ, and who lived in the time of the Apostles, that the Jews acknowledged no books as Divine, but twenty-two. " We have not," he says, " an innumerable multitude of books among us, disagreeing from, and contradicting one another, (as the Greeks have,) but only twenty-two books, which contain the records of all the past times; which are justly believed to be Divine. And of them five belong to Moses, which contain his laws, and the traditions of the origin of mankind till his death. This interval of time was little short of 3000 years. But as to the time from the death of Moses till the reign of Artaxerxes King of Persia, who reigned after Xerxes, the prophets, who were after Moses, wrote down what was done in their times in thirteen books. The remaining four books contain hymns to God, and precepts for the conduct of human life. It is true, our history hath been written since Artaxerxes very particularly, but hath not been esteemed of the like authority with the former by our forefathers, because there hath not been an exact succession of prophets since that time : And how firmly we have given credit to these books of our own nation, is evident by what we do ; for during so many ages as have already passed, no one hath been so bold as either to add any thing to them, to take any thing from them, or to make any change in them ; but it is become natural to all Jews, immediately, and from their very birth, to esteem these books to contain Divine doctrines, and to persist in them, and, if occasion be, willingly to die for them."—Josephus, ed. 1784, vol. ii. 361. The books here referred to are precisely the same, that from the beginning have been received by Christians, and that are still acknowledged by the modern Jews, concerning whose undivided attachment to them, all that is here asserted by Josephus is verified to the present day.

The authenticity of the Old Testament Scriptures, against which there is no contradictory testimony, is confirmed by many collateral evidences of customs, traditions, and natural appearances, that have been collected from every part of the world. It is likewise supported by all the notices to be found respecting them in the most ancient heathen historians. Josephus appeals to the public records of different nations, and to a great number of books extant in his time, but now lost, as indisputable evidence, in the opinion of the Heathen world, for the truth of the most remarkable events related in his History, the account of the early periods of which he professes to have taken principally from the Pentateuch. Porphyry, one of the most acute and learned of the early enemies of Christianity, admitted the genuineness of the Pentateuch, and acknowledged that Moses was prior to the Phœnician Sanchoniathon, who lived before the Trojan war. He even contended for the truth of Sanchoniathon's account of the Jews, from its coincidence with the Mosaic history. Nor was the genuineness of the Pentateuch denied, by any of the numerous writers against the Gospel, in the four first centuries, although the Christian fathers constantly appealed to the history and prophecies of the Old Testament in support of the Divine origin of the doctrines which they taught. The power of historical truth compelled the Emperor Julian, whose favour to the Jews appears to have proceeded only from his hostility to the Christians, to acknowledge, that persons instructed by the Spirit of God once lived among the Israelites; and to confess that the books which bore the name of Moses were genuine; and that the facts which they contained were worthy of credit.

Of the genuineness and authenticity of their Scriptures, the Jews had the strongest evidence, which produced a corresponding impression. The five books of Moses are addressed to the Israelites as his contemporaries, and had they not been both genuine and authentic, they never could have been imposed on his countrymen, whose religion and government were founded upon them. The transactions of their own times were narrated by the several writers of the other books, and the truth of their respective histories was witnessed by all their countrymen who lived at the same period. The plainest directions were given for ascertaining the truth of the mission of all who declared themselves prophets, those who were sent being furnished with ample credentials, while every one who pretended to deliver the messages of God, without these credentials, was to be put to death. Deut. xviii. 20. And although false prophets did arise, and for a time obtained a degree of influence, their wickedness was exposed by the failure of their predictions, or by the judgments inflicted on them, as in the case of Hananiah. From the miracles, too, which the people of Israel constantly witnessed, as well as the fulfilment of the prophecies all along taking place, they had complete proof that the true prophets wrote by the authority of God himself. During the whole period from Moses to Malachi, a succession of them was raised up, under whose direction the Word of God was infallibly distinguished from all counterfeits; and by their means, in connexion with the visible interference of the God of Israel in punishing those who made the people trust in a lie, the Scriptures were preserved pure and unadulterated.

These books are handed down to us by that nation, whose history they record with an impartiality for which we shall seek in vain in the annals of any other historians. There are here no national prejudices, and no attempts at embellishment. The history of the people of Israel is recorded by the uncompromising hand of truth. Their ingratitude, and their obstinacy, are alike exposed; their sinful incredulity on many occasions is published; their virtues are not magnified, and their courage is not extolled. This history contains an account, not in confused traditions, but in minute detail of time, place, and circumstances, of great public facts transacted in the presence of the whole people, in which they were actors, and of which permanent memorials were instituted at the time when they occurred.*

---

* Mr Leslie, who writes on Deism, in proving the authenticity of the books of Moses, lays down the following rules as a test of truth, which all meet in these books. Wherever they do meet, what they refer to, he affirms, cannot be false. On the contrary, they cannot possibly meet in any imposture whatever.

" 1. That the matter of fact be such, that men's outward senses, their eyes and ears, may be judges of it.

" 2. That it be done publicly in the face of the world.

" 3. That not only public monuments be kept in memory of it, but some outward actions be performed.

" 4 That such monuments, and such actions, or observances, be instituted, and do commence from the time that the matter of fact was done.

" The two first rules make it impossible for any such matter of fact to be imposed on men at the time when said to be done, because every man's eyes and senses would contradict it. The two last rules render it impossible that the matter of fact should be invented and imposed some time after."

After proving, in a variety of ways, that all his four rules meet in the books of Moses, he observes:—" You may challenge the

These facts involved their submission to a religion entirely different from that of all the surrounding nations, which laid them under great and painful restraints, and to laws and institutions, which, while they secluded them from the rest of mankind, exposed them to their utmost detestation and contempt. Had such facts never taken place, they could not at any period have been forced upon the belief of a whole nation, so as to be ever afterwards acknowledged by them, *without one dissenting voice.* It is a striking singularity in their laws, that they were promulgated not from time to time, but in one written code, and were permanently binding both on the rulers and the people, never to be in any respect either altered or enlarged.

Nor are the Jews alone referred to as witnesses of some of the most important of those transactions, the scene of which is not laid in an obscure corner, but in the midst of the most civilized nations of the world. The entrance of their ancestors into Egypt; their continuance for centuries, and increase there; the manner in which they were oppressed; the causes of their being suffered to depart, and the awful catas-

---

whole world to show any action that is fabulous, which has all the four rules or marks before mentioned. *It is impossible.*—I do not say that every thing which wants these four marks is false, but that *nothing can be false which has them all.*"

It is said that Dr Middleton endeavoured for twenty years to find out some pretended fact to which Mr Leslie's four rules could be applied, but without success.

trophe which accompanied that departure,—are facts in which the people of Egypt were equally implicated with themselves. Their subsequent continuance during forty years in an uncultivated desert; their invasion of Palestine; the long-continued contest, and their final occupation of that land,—were public and permanent facts, brought home to the inhabitants of that country, who lived in the centre of the civilized world. The train of the history too, which, as well as the style and tendency of all the separate books, is entirely consistent with itself, proceeds in so uniform a manner, and one thing so naturally rises out of another, that unless on the supposition of what goes before, that which follows cannot be accounted for. This remark holds good with respect to the state of the Jews even to this day; and all that is recorded is necessary to explain their present unexampled situation. Impressed with an unalterable conviction of their Divine origin, they have, at the expense of every thing dear to men, tenaciously adhered, as far as circumstances permit, to the outward form of the religion, the laws, and the institutions engrossed in their sacred records. And although they themselves are condemned by these books, and know that they are employed to support a system which they mortally hate, they have, under all circumstances, down to the present hour, continued to be faithful depositaries of the Old Testament Scriptures.

"The honour and privilege," says Bishop Cosin, in his History of the Canon of the Holy Scripture, "which the posterity of Jacob sometime had, above all the world besides, was to be that peculiar people of God, to whom he was pleased to make his laws and his Scriptures known; nor was there then any other church but theirs, or any other oracles of God, than what were committed to them. For they had all that were then extant, and all written in their own language.

"These they divided into three several classes, whereof the first comprehended THE FIVE BOOKS OF MOSES; the second ALL THE PROPHETS; and the third *those* WRITINGS which they call the *Chethubim*, or BOOKS that were written by the holy men of God, who were not so properly to be ranked among the Prophets: From whom both the *five Books of Moses* and these *Chethubim* were distinguished, because howsoever they were all written by the same prophetical spirit and instinct which the *Books of the Prophets* were, yet *Moses* having been their special lawgiver, and the *writers of these other books* having had no public mission or office of *Prophets*, (for some of them were *Kings*, and others were *great and potent persons* in their times,) they gave either of them a *peculiar class* by themselves.

"In this division, as they reckoned *Five Books* in the first class, so in the second they counted *Eight*, and in the third *Nine; Two-and-Twenty* in all; in number equal to the letters of their *Alphabet*, and as fully comprehending all that was then needful to be known and believed, as the number of their letters did all that was requisite to be said or written. And hereof after this manner they made their enumeration:

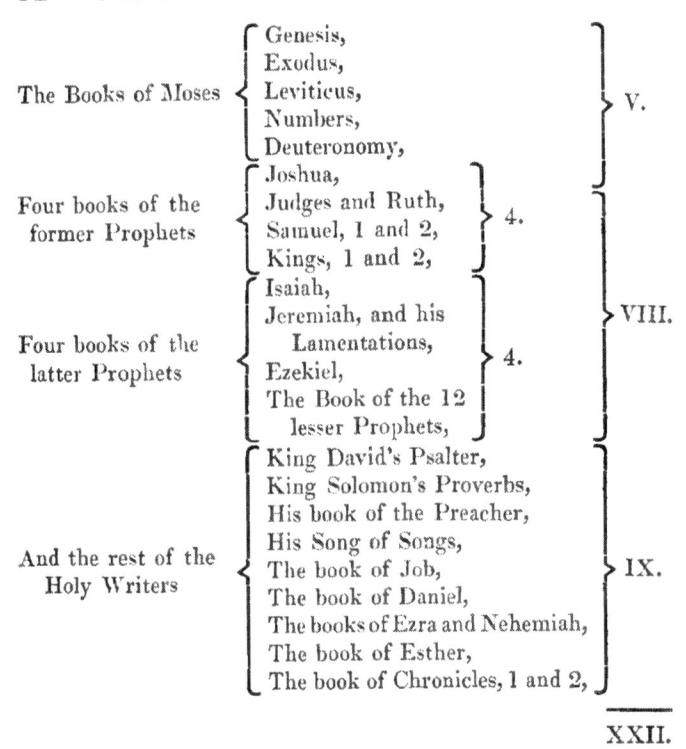

The Books of Moses	{ Genesis, Exodus, Leviticus, Numbers, Deuteronomy, }	V.
Four books of the former Prophets	{ Joshua, Judges and Ruth, Samuel, 1 and 2, Kings, 1 and 2, } 4.	
Four books of the latter Prophets	{ Isaiah, Jeremiah, and his Lamentations, Ezekiel, The Book of the 12 lesser Prophets, } 4.	VIII.
And the rest of the Holy Writers	{ King David's Psalter, King Solomon's Proverbs, His book of the Preacher, His Song of Songs, The book of Job, The book of Daniel, The books of Ezra and Nehemiah, The book of Esther, The book of Chronicles, 1 and 2, }	IX.

XXII.

" Which last *Book of the Chronicles*, containing the sum of all their former histories, and reaching from the creation of the world to their return from *Babylon*, is a perfect *epitome of all the old Testament*, and therefore not unfitly so placed by them, as that it concluded and closed up their whole BIBLE.

" Other *divisions* of these books were afterwards made, and the *order* of them was somewhat altered, (as in divers respects they may well be,) but the books were still the *same;* and as the *number* of them was never augmented, during the time of the Old Testament, so there were no *additional pieces* brought in, or set to any of them at all.

"It is generally received, that after the return of the Jews from their captivity in *Babylon*, all the BOOKS of the SCRIPTURE, having been revised by *Ezra*, (then their priest and their leader,) who digested them likewise into those several classes before rehearsed, were by him, and the Prophets of God that lived with him, consigned and delivered over to all posterity. But this is sure, that after his age, and the time of the prophet *Malachi*, (who was *one* among those that prophesied in that time,) there were no more *prophets* heard of among the Jews till the time of St John the Baptist, and therefore no more prophetical and divine SCRIPTURES between them.

"The BOOKS then of the OLD TESTAMENT, such and so many as they were after the captivity of Babylon, in the time of *Esdras*, (Ezra,) the same and so many being accurately preserved by the *Jews*, and continuing among them unto the time of our *blessed Saviour* (as they do likewise still unto this very day) without any addition, imminution, or alteration, descended to the *Christians*."

Nothing then can be better authenticated than the canon* of the Old Testament, as we now possess it.

---

* The word canon signifies a rule or a law. Hence the books of the Holy Scriptures, taken together, are called the Canon, as designed by God to be the rule of our faith and practice.

We have the fullest evidence that it was fixed 280 years before the Christian era, when, as has been noticed, the Greek translation, called the Septuagint, was executed at Alexandria, the books of which were the same as in our Bible. And as no authentic records of a more ancient date are extant, it is impossible to ascend higher in search of testimony. As held by the Jews in the days of Jesus Christ, their canon was the same as when that translation was made, and it has since then been retained by them without any variation, though by separating books formerly united, they increase their number. The integrity and Divine original of these Scriptures are thus authenticated by a whole nation —the most ancient that exists—who have preserved them, and borne their testimony to them, from the time of Moses down to the present day. That nation was selected by God himself to be his witnesses, Isaiah, xliii. 10, to whom he committed "the lively oracles," and amidst all their wickedness he prevented them from betraying their trust, the Jews never having given admission into their canon to any other books but to those which by his prophets and servants were delivered to them.

In addition to the unanimous testimony of the Jewish nation to the genuineness and authenticity of the Old Testament Scriptures, of which they had been constituted the depositaries, we have the decisive attestation of the Son of God. Jesus Christ, who appeared on earth 1500 years after Moses, the first of the prophets, and 400 years after Malachi, the last of them, bore his testimony to the sacred canon as held by the Jews in his time, and recorded it by his holy Apostles. Among all the evils with which he charged the Jews, he never once intimated that they had in any degree corrupted the canon, either by addition, or diminution, or alteration. Since with so much zeal he purged the temple, and so often and sharply reprehended the Jews, for perverting the true sense of the Scriptures, much more, we may be assured, would he have condemned them, if they had tampered with, or vitiated, these sacred writings; but of this he never accused them. By often referring to the " Scriptures," which he declared " cannot be broken," the Lord Jesus Christ has given his full attestation to the whole of them as the unadulterated Word of God. *" Search the Scriptures, for in them ye think ye have eternal life, and they are they which testify of me."* Here he warrants, in the most explicit manner, the canon of the Hebrew Scriptures. He told the Jews that they *made the Word of God of none effect through their traditions.* By calling them the WORD OF GOD, he indicated that these Scriptures proceeded from God himself. In his conversation with the disciples going to Emaus, when, *" beginning at Moses and all the Prophets, he expounded to them in all the Scriptures the things concerning himself,"* he gave the most express testimony to every one of the books of the Old Testament canon. Just before his ascension, he said to his Apostles, *" These are the words which I spake unto you while I was yet with you, that all things must be fulfilled which were written in the law of Moses, and in the Prophets, and in the Psalms, concerning me."* By thus adopting the common division of the Law, and the Prophets, and the Psalms, which comprehended all the Hebrew Scriptures, (to which division Josephus, as we have seen, refers,) he ratified and sanctioned by his authority the canon of the Old Testament, as it was received by the Jews; and by declaring that these books contained prophecies that must be fulfilled, he established their Divine inspiration, since God alone can enable men to foretell future events.

The same testimony is repeated by the Apostles, who constantly appeal to the Jewish Scriptures as *"the lively oracles"* of God. Referring to the *whole* of the Old Testament, Paul declares, that *"All Scripture is given by inspiration of God."* The term "Scripture," or "the Scriptures," (the writings,) was then, as it is still, appropriated to the written Word of God, as both the Old Testament and the New are now, by way of eminence and distinction, called the *Bible,* or the Book. The same Apostle recognises the entire canon of the Jews, when he says, *"unto them were committed the oracles of God."* The fidelity of the Jews to their trust is here asserted by Paul; and those to whom he writes are required to acknowledge the Scriptures of the Old Testament as of Divine authority. While the Apostles affirmed that they spoke *" not the words which man's wisdom teacheth, but which the Holy Ghost teacheth,"* they uniformly referred to the Old Testament Scriptures, as of equal authority with those of the New Testament, both of which, as commissioned by their Divine Master, they have delivered over to the Christian Church as "the Word of God." Indeed, so manifestly is it the object of the Apostles to establish the Divine authority of the Old Testament, that though they were as fully inspired and accredited as the ancient prophets, or former servants of God, and could establish the truth of any thing they taught by the miracles which they performed, yet they reasoned out of the Old Testament Scriptures, proving and alleging from them the truth of what they declared. Instead of professing to give authority to what was written in them, they uniformly appealed to those writings as authority equal to their own. Paul declares, that the Gospel of God, to which he was separated as an Apostle, was that *"which he had promised afore by his prophets in the Holy Scriptures,"*—Rom, 1, 2.*

---

* Much important matter is contained in this verse. The Apostle here tacitly repels the accusation of the Jews, that the Gospel was a novel doctrine. He shows that the Old Testament is the promise of the New, and that the New is the fulfilment of the Old—by its prophecies which foretold a new covenant—by all that it promised concerning the Messiah—by all its legal institutions which contained in themselves the promises which they prefigured—by the whole economy of the law which prepared men for the reception of the Gospel—by all the revelations of grace and mercy which contained the Gospel in substance, and, consequently, promised its more full developement. He also repels the accusation, that the Apostles were enemies to Moses and the Prophets; showing, on the other hand, that there was a complete agreement betwixt them. He establishes the authority of the prophets and the inspiration of the Scriptures, by decla-

Here, where Paul asserts his Apostolic commission, he gives the whole weight of his Apostolic authority to the ancient Scriptures, which he denominates " Holy writings," in which God, he affirms, had recorded his promises by his prophets. When the same Apostle declares, that "*whatsoever things were written afore time were written for our learning; that we, through patience and comfort of the Scriptures, might have hope,*" he gives his attestation to the whole of the sacred writings, and proves that they exist entire; for he could not have said this if any of them had been lost,* or had any additions been made to them.

---

ring that it was God himself who spoke in them., He shows whence we are to take the true Word of God and of his prophets, not from verbal tradition, which must be uncertain and fluctuating, but from the written Word, which is certain and permanent. He teaches that we ought constantly to have recourse to the Scriptures, for that all in religion which is not found in them, is really novel, although it may have been received for many ages; but that what is found there is really ancient, although men may have for a long time lost sight of it. Such are the great truths contained in this compendious verse.

* It is true, that the sacred writers refer to other books that do not now exist, as of Iddo the seer, but they do not refer to them as canonical books, but as civil records of the kingdom, such as the reference to the civil records of Persia in the book of Esther. Were it even to be admitted that some epistles written by the Apostles have not come down to us, the fact would not imply that the Scriptures have lost an epistle, or a single word. There might have been hundreds of such inspired letters from the Apostles, without implying that ever they made a part of that collection

From the important connexion that subsists between the Old Testament and the New, the early Christian writers carefully examined the Jewish Scriptures, and have given distinct catalogues of these books, precisely the same as we now receive, and as they are still retained by the Jews. Melito, Bishop of Sardis, travelled in the second century into Palestine, on purpose to investigate the subject. His catalogue, which is preserved by Eusebius, contains the canonical books of the Old Testament, and no more. He names the several books, comprehending under the Book of Ezra, those of Nehemiah and Esther, to which they were commonly annexed, these three being by many accounted but one book. In the Jewish list, the Book of Nehemiah, only, was joined to Esther, as the Book of Lamentations was also annexed to Jeremiah; but the Book of Esther was never wanting in the canon of the Jews. The learned Origen, in the third century, gives a catalogue of the Jewish Scriptures, and says, " that the canonical books of Scripture contained in the Old Testament,

---

that was designed by God to be a perfect and sufficient standard to all ages. This is said not from a conviction that there ever existed any inspired letters of the Apostles except those which we possess,* but they may have existed in any number without affecting the integrity of the Canon, which some have weakly supposed would follow from the fact, if admitted.

* " Some," says Theodoret, " imagine Paul to have wrote an epistle to the Laodiceans, and accordingly produce a certain forged epistle (so entitled); but the Holy Apostle does not say τὴν πρὸς Λαοδικείας the epistle *to* the Laodiceans, but τὴν ἐκ Λαοδικείας, the epistle *from* the Laodiceans."

are twenty and two in number, which the Hebrews have left unto us, according to the number of letters which they have in their alphabet." Athanasius also, in the fourth century, specifies the twenty-two books, and, naming them one after another, in the same order in which they now stand, says, that " they are received by the whole church." Hilary of Poictiers, and many writers in the same century, affirm that these books alone were received as canonical. This fact is confirmed by the Council of Laodicea, which met in the year 363, and gave a list of the twenty-two books, the same as have been received both by Jews and Christians.

Nothing can be more satisfactory and conclusive than all the parts of the foregoing evidence of the authenticity and integrity of the Canon of the Old Testament Scriptures. The Jews, to whom they were first committed, never varied respecting them; while they have been fully recognised by the Lord and his Apostles, and consequently, their authenticity is established by express revelation. And that we now possess them as thus delivered and authenticated, we have the concurrent testimony of the whole succession of the most distinguished early Christian writers, as well as of the Jews to this day, who, in every age, and in all countries, the most remote from one another, have constantly been in use of reading them in their synagogues.

The Scriptures of the Old Testament that have been thus so faithfully preserved, and so fully attested, contain the most satisfactory and convincing internal evidences of their truth. The character of God which they exhibit, nowhere delineated in the writings of any of the wisest of this world, unenlightened by revelation, is such as carries with it its own confirmation. The character they give of man is verified in the history of every nation, and of each individual. The majesty, purity, and suitableness to the condition of man, of the doctrine they contain—the soundness and unrivalled excellence of the moral precepts they inculcate, and the glory of the succeeding dispensation which, towards their close, they point out with increasing clearness; and all this confirmed and verified in the minutest particulars by the New Testament Scriptures—form a body of internal evidence to which nothing but the deep corruption of the human heart, and the enmity of the carnal mind against God, could render any one insensible.

In course of time, and in the progress of that corruption in the churches which soon began to work, the sacred canon was defiled by the addition and even intermixture of other books, which, through the unfaithfulness of Christians, were admitted first as of secondary, and at length by many as of equal authority and consideration with those of which it was composed.

These books were called Apocryphal, and are supposed to have been so denominated from the Greek word ἀποκρυπτω, *to hide—to conceal*, which is expressive of the uncertainty and concealed nature of their origin. Who their authors were is not known. They were written subsequently to the cessation of the prophetic spirit in the time of Malachi, who closed his testimony by reminding the people of Israel of the authority of the law of Moses, and intimating that after himself, no prophet was to arise until the harbinger of the Messiah should appear. They were not written in the Hebrew language, in which all the books of the Old Testament were originally composed, with the exception of a few passages in Jeremiah, Daniel, Ezra, and Esther, which were written in Chaldee. Both Philo and Josephus, who flourished in the first century of the Christian era, are altogether silent concerning these spurious books, which were not contained in the Septuagint version, as set forth by the translators under Ptolemy;* and they form no part of those sacred writings committed by God to the Jews, universally acknowledged and preserved by them entire. Above all, they have not received, like these holy writings, the attestation of Jesus Christ, and his Apostles, placing upon them the broad seal of heaven, by whom they have never once

---

* " Of the *Greek Septuagint Bible*, (as it was first set forth in the time of Ptolemæus Philadelphus,) *St Augustin* acknowledged no more *Books*, than what were then translated out of the *Hebrew copies* sent from *Jerusalem*, where neither *Tobit* nor *Judith*, nor any of that *class*, were to be found ; for (whatever *Genebrard* saith of his own head to the contrary,) those *additional writings* were brought in afterwards, and used only by the *Hellenist Jews* abroad at *Babylon* and *Alexandria*, from whom they were, in time following, commended to be read by the *Christians*, but never made *equal* with the *other sacred Scriptures*, as they are now set forth in the *Roman Septuagint* by the authority of *Sixtus Quintus*, which is an addition of *that Bible*, many ways depraved."—Cosin, p. 98.

been quoted. A real and essential difference was constantly maintained by the early Christians between them and the canonical books; and it was not till the fourth century, when the churches had become exceedingly corrupt both in faith and practice, that they came to be permitted to appear with the canon.

The Apocryphal books, though not admitted by the first Christian writers, or churches, to have any authority in matters of faith, yet claim for themselves that authority, and even arrogate an equality with the sacred Scriptures, to which they were at length advanced by the church of Rome. They present themselves to the world as a part of the Word of God, sometimes communicated immediately by himself, sometimes conveyed through the medium of angels, who are represented as standing before him. The claim to inspiration is not more explicitly asserted by the writers of the Scriptures, than by some of the authors of the Apocryphal books. No higher demand for attention to their messages can be made by holy prophets and apostles, than when they affirm, " Thus saith the Lord." Yet this is the language in which men are addressed by these authors. They *" have daubed them with untempered mortar, seeing vanity, and divining lies unto them,* SAYING, THUS SAITH THE LORD GOD, *when the Lord hath not spoken."* Ezek. xxii. 28.

In the second book of Esdras, the writer having commenced by declaring his lineage, affirms, " *The word of the Lord came unto me, saying*, Go thy way and show my people, &c." " Speak thou therefore unto them, saying, *Thus saith the Lord.*"—

"*Thus saith the Almighty Lord.*" This expression occurs four times in the first chapter. The second chapter opens with "*Thus saith the Lord,*" which in the course of that chapter is repeated nine times, and an angel is represented as speaking to the writer. "*Then the angel said unto me,* go thy way, and tell my people what manner of things, and how great wonders of the Lord thy God thou hast seen." The rest of the book proceeds in the same strain, the author pretending to recite Divine communications, made to himself as had been made to Moses.

In the Book of Baruch, ii. 21, it is written, "*Thus saith the Lord.*"

In the book of Tobit a long interview with an angel is related, who affirms that he is one of the holy angels who go in and out before the glory of the Holy One. "Now, therefore," says this angel, "give God thanks, for I go up to him that sent me, but write all things which are done in a book." Tobit, xii. 15, 20. God himself is often introduced by the Apocryphal writers, as communicating his will to them, and long speeches are ascribed to the Almighty.* Thus, the writers of the Apocrypha come as the bearers of messages from God, and as such they deliver them to mankind. They profess to communicate a portion of spiritual light, not borrowed from the Holy Scriptures, but immediately derived from the source

---

* The absurd, unintelligible speeches, replete with trifling nonsense, ascribed to God in different places, prove the Apocrypha to be not only a human, but a most *impious* composition.

of light. In every sense of the word, these books present themselves as a part of Divine Revelation, and if they were what they pretend to be, would be entitled to equal attention and reverence with the Holy Scriptures. Here, then, there is no medium, and the conclusion is inevitable :—*The Apocrypha is either an addition made to the Old Testament Scriptures by God himself, or it is the work of lying prophets.* This important question ought, therefore, to be considered by every Christian, and happily its solution is attended with no difficulty.

The Hebrew Scriptures come to us, as we have seen, with the fullest and most unequivocal attestations, that they are the oracles of God. On the other hand, if we examine the claim of the Apocryphal books, what do we observe? External evidence of their constituting a portion of Divine Revelation they have none. The question, then, on this ground alone, even were there no other to which we could appeal, is for ever decided against them. But in order to produce the fullest conviction in the minds of all who know the truth as it is in Jesus, and to exclude every doubt, let us call another witness. We shall appeal, then, to the internal evidence of these writings. They contain within themselves their own condemnation. They are inconsistent, absurd, and contrary to the Word of God.

Viewing the Apocryphal writings as added to the Holy Scriptures, what character do they present? Do they offer any thing new, any thing that it might be of importance to know beyond what is contained in the Scriptures of the Old and New Testaments?

Do they teach us the way of God more perfectly? This will not be pretended by any one. Do their histories, which they present to us as true, comport with the dignity of Holy Writ? Do they possess internal marks of being authentic? Do they bear the character of a revelation from God, given for our instruction? So far is this from being the case, that many of their narrations are incredible and self-contradictory, and others irreconcilably at variance with the canonical Scriptures. They are defiled with a variety of errors, vanities, low conceits, and other faults incident to human nature and human infirmity. While their style, far different from the grave and chaste simplicity, or the divine and spiritual majesty, of the pure genuine Word of God, is deformed with levity, and affectation of worldly wisdom and eloquence.

The Apocryphal books are not only replete with absurdities, superstitions, and falsehoods, in their narrations, but also with false doctrines directly opposed to the doctrine of the Holy Scriptures, such as those of purgatory and prayers for the dead. But waving for the present every other charge against them on this head, let us turn our attention to a single point of the last importance, which involves an answer to that most momentous of all questions, *How shall man be just before God?* The Scriptures assure us, that if any man denies the doctrine of justification by faith without works, he becomes a debtor to do the whole law. What judgment then are we bound to form of a book which, openly contradicting this fundamental doctrine, and exhibiting another way of acceptance with God, makes void the whole plan of redemption? On this one point, then, of the explicit contravention by the Apocryphal books of the grand Scripture doctrine of justification, let them be tried;—that doctrine which is peculiar to the Christian religion, and unknown to every false one, and which so remarkably illustrates and honours the finished work of the Redeemer—that doctrine of which God in his word has affirmed of the man who perverts it, that Christ shall profit him nothing.

It is written in the Apocrypha, "*Whoso honoureth his father maketh an atonement for his sins;*" and again, "*Water will quench a flaming fire, and alms maketh an atonement for sins.*" Eccl. iii. 3—30. Sentiments more directly opposed to the doctrine of the Holy Scriptures, more dishonourable to God, more contrary to his *holiness*, more derogatory to his *justice*, or more fraught with mortal poison, and more destructive to the souls of men, cannot be conceived.

The Apostle Paul solemnly declared to the churches of Galatia, that if an angel from heaven should preach any other gospel than that which he had preached unto them, he should be accursed. That very occurrence which the Apostle thus supposes, has, according to the Apocrypha, been realized. An angel from heaven, it affirms, has descended and declared that he came from God. "*I am Raphael, one of the seven holy angels, which present the prayers of the saints, and which go in and out before the glory of the Holy One; not of any favour of mine, but by the will of our God I came."* Tobit, xii. 15, 18. And that very doctrine does this angel flatly contradict which the Apostle so earnestly inculcated, accompanied with the solemn asseveration, that the curse of God should rest on any creature who dared to pervert it. "*It is better,*" says this angel, "*to give alms than to lay up gold: for alms doth deliver from death, and shall purge away all sin.*" Tobit, xii. 8, 9. If the man or angel who shall preach another gospel than that which the Bible contains, is pronounced by the Holy Ghost to be accursed, then must this awful denunciation apply to a book, which, pretending to record the message of an angel from heaven, teaches another gospel. On the Apocrypha, therefore, does this anathema rest.

The writers, then, of the Apocryphal books, " who tread down the pastures, and foul the residue of the waters with their feet," (Ezek. xxxiv. 18,) are, by confronting their doctrine with that of the holy Apostles, proved to be false prophets, against whom the wrath of God and many woes are denounced in Scripture. In opposition to their folly and wickedness, the Lord says, " The prophet that hath a dream, let him tell a dream; and he that hath my word, let him speak my word faithfully. What is the chaff to the wheat? saith the Lord. Is not my word like as a fire? saith the Lord; and like a hammer that breaketh the rock in pieces?" Jer. xxii. 28.— " The prophet, which shall presume to speak a word in my name, which I have not commanded him to speak, or that shall speak in the name of other gods, even that prophet shall die." Deut. xviii. 20. These, and many other passages, are pointedly applicable to the Apocrypha. The writers of it may be justly termed prophets of deceit, and of their own heart, that prophesy lies in the name of the Lord, " *saying, I have dreamed, I have dreamed.*" Jer. xxiii. 25. They have indeed imitated the style of the Scriptures, like the impostors concerning whom it is written, " Therefore, behold I am against the prophets, saith the Lord, that steal my words every one from his neighbour. Behold I am against the prophets, saith the Lord, that use their tongues, and say, He saith. Behold, I am against them that prophesy false dreams, saith the Lord, and do tell them, and cause my people to err by their lies, and by their lightness; yet I sent them not, nor commanded them: therefore they shall not profit this people at all, saith the Lord." Jer. xxiii. 30. " Thus saith the Lord God; Woe unto the foolish prophets, that follow their own spirit, and have seen nothing !— Have ye not seen a vain vision, and have ye not spoken a lying divination, whereas ye say, The Lord saith it; albeit I have not spoken? Therefore, thus saith the Lord God; Because ye have spoken vanity, and seen lies, therefore, behold I am against you, saith the Lord God. And mine hand shall be upon the prophets that see vanity, and that divine lies." Ezek. xiii. 3, 7, 9. The Bible then, and the Apocrypha, stand in direct opposition in their doctrine, and the latter is denounced by the former, and lies under its heaviest anathemas. The Apocryphal books, when delivered to the people as part of the Divine oracles, are calculated by their absurdities to make men Deists or Atheists rather than Christians, and by their false doctrines to cause their readers to wrest the Scriptures to their own destruction. As their introduction into the sacred canon has been the grand and crowning device of Satan for deceiving and corrupting the Christian world, and supporting the claims of the mother of harlots and abominations of the earth, it will be proper to trace it from its origin.

Although all the Apocryphal books had been called, by the first Christian writers, spurious and supposititious, as not being inspired, but, on the contrary, containing doctrines which subvert the very foundations of the Gospel, and of a sinner's acceptance before God; yet some of them were at length selected as being supposed to be purer than the rest, and better entitled to be used in public readings and services, and on this account they received the name of Ecclesiastical or Church books. Of these there was even formed a register or inferior canon, to exclude such as were reckoned more erroneous or faulty; and this, in process of time, occasioned the name of canonical to be given in common to the writings which were truly Divine, and to those which were reckoned the best of the Apocryphal books. The books of the first canon were esteemed to be divinely inspired, and to be the certain rule of faith. The Apocryphal books were reckoned to be instructive and useful, but were excluded from all authority in matters of faith, and in determination of controversies; and when they came to be permitted to be read in the churches, the reader stood up in an inferior place.* It happened, however, in the course of years, that all these Canonical and Apocryphal books were conjoined and bound up together in one volume, for the greater facility of ecclesiastical use ; and for the purpose of uniting the historical parts with the historical, the proverbial with the proverbial, the doctrinal with the doctrinal, they were *intermingled* with one another, as at present in the Roman Catholic Bibles. But this practice obtained no sanction from the primitive churches, or the best and earliest of the Christian fathers, who, on the contrary, strongly objected against it ; and denied that these books were possessed of any authority. At the beginning they were not acknowledged at all, nor admitted into any of the earlier catalogues of the Scriptures, and their introduction to that place which they afterwards unlawfully usurped, was slow and partial.

Justin, who suffered martyrdom for the Christian faith, in the year 163, never, in any of his writings, cites a single passage of the Apocryphal books, nor makes the least mention of them in his conference

---

* Augustine, who lived in the fifth century, relates, that when the Book of Wisdom, and other writings of the same class, were publicly read in the church, they were given to the readers or inferior ecclesiastical officers, who read them in a place lower than that in which those universally acknowledged to be the canonical, were read by the bishops and presbyters in a more eminent and conspicuous manner.

with Trypho : while he speaks of it as a special work of Divine Providence, that the Jews had been faithful preservers of the Scriptures. None of these books appear in the catalogue of the Old Testament Scriptures of Melito, Bishop of Sardis, in the second century ; nor in that of Origen, in the third century.

In the fourth century, Eusebius, who was Bishop of Cæsarea in the year 320, affirms, that from the time of Jesus Christ, there were no sacred books of Holy Scripture, besides those which had been received into the canon of the Jewish and Christian churches. He had read the Apocryphal books, and makes frequent quotations from them as the writings of particular authors, but never acknowledges any of them as a part of the canonical Scriptures. He declares that the authors of those books which bear the names of the Wisdom of Solomon, and the Wisdom of the Son of Sirach, are writers contradicted, or not allowed, in the canon. When Porphyry adduced some objections against him from the new pieces annexed to the book of Daniel, he said that he was not bound to defend them, because they had no authority of Holy Scripture.

In the year 325, the first general council was held at Nice, at which were present 318 bishops, besides multitudes of other Christians, from all the provinces and churches of the Roman Empire. That in the Scriptures they made use of, " there were none of the controverted books, appears," says Bishop Cosin, p. 42, " by the evidence and attestation which both the Emperor Eusebius, and Athanasius, (the chiefest actors in this council,) have hereunto given us."

Athanasius, who flourished in the year 340, enumerates the books of the Old and New Testament precisely as we now have them, and asserts that these alone are to be accounted the canonical and authentic sacred writings, admitted by the Lord and his Apostles, and recognised by all the fathers and teachers of the church since the Apostolic age. At the same time he reproves those who had intermixed a number of the Apocryphal books with the catalogue of the acknowledged books of the Old Testament.

"These things," says Cyril, who was Bishop of Jerusalem in the year 350, "we are taught by the divinely-inspired Scriptures of the Old and New Testaments. For there is one God of both Testaments, who in the Old Testament foretold the Christ, who was manifested in the New.—Read the Divine Scriptures, the two-and-twenty books of the Old Testament, which were translated by the seventy-two interpreters—Read these two-and-twenty books, and have nothing to do with Apocryphal writings. These and these only, do you carefully meditate upon, which we securely or openly read in the church. The Apostles and ancient bishops, governors of the church, who have delivered them to us, were wiser and holier men than thou. As a son of the church, therefore, transgress not these bounds; meditate upon the books of the Old Testament, which, as has been already said, are two-and-twenty ; and if you are desirous to learn, fix them in your memory, as I enumerate them, one by one." The list of these books Cyril subjoins; it is precisely the same as the Jewish canon which we receive.*

The council of Laodicea, which met in the year 363, prohibited the public reading of any books as sacred or inspired, except the canonical. In their 59th canon, it is declared, " that private psalms ought not to be read (or said) in the church, nor any books not canonical, but only the canonical books of the Old and New Testament."

" The Hebrews," says Jerom, who was ordained presbyter of Antioch about the year 378, " have two-and-twenty letters, and they have as many books of divine doctrine for the instruction of mankind." He next gives a list of these books, and then adds, " This prologue I write as a preface to all the books to be translated by me from the Hebrew into Latin, that we may know that all the books that are not of this

---

* "—although both *he* (Cyril) at *Jerusalem*, and *Athanasius* at *Alexandria*, together with *other churches*, had not the use of the *Hebrew Bible* among them, but kept themselves only to the *Greek translation* of the LXX., whereunto were afterwards commonly added those *ecclesiastical books* which the *Hellenist Jews* first introduced, and received into their churches, that so all the most eminent books of religion written in the Greek tongue before *Christ's* time might be put together and contained in *one volume*; yet nevertheless they were always careful to preserve the honour of the *Hebrew canon*, which consisted of XXII. books only, *divinely inspired*; and accurately to distinguish them from the *rest*, which had but *ecclesiastical authority*."—Cosin, p. 54.

number, are to be reckoned Apocryphal. Therefore Wisdom, which is commonly called Solomon's, and the book of Jesus the son of Sirach, and Judith, and Tobit, and the Shepherd, are not in the canon." In his Latin translation, called the Vulgate, Jerom intermingled the Apocryphal and inspired writings, but, to prevent mistake, he prefixed to each book a short notice, in which the reader was distinctly informed of its character, and apprized that the Apocryphal writings were not in the canon of Scripture. He says that to meet the prejudices of the ignorant, he retained these " fables," which, though not in the Hebrew, were widely dispersed; but he adds, that, according to his custom, he had marked these Apocryphal intruders with a spit or dagger, placed horizontally for the purpose of stabbing them.* In his letter to Læta, written about the year 398, giving her instructions concerning her daughter Paula, he advises that she should read the Scriptures, and in this order: first the Psalms, next the Proverbs, the Acts, and the Epistles of the Apostles. Afterwards

---

* After the third verse of the tenth chapter of Esther, where the Apocryphal addition to that book commences, Jerom has inserted the following notice; it is the ancient Vulgate to which he refers, which was the most common version of his time :—
" Quæ habentur in Hebræo, plena fide expressi. Hæc autem, quæ sequuntur, scripta reperi in editione vulgata, quæ Græcorum lingua et literis continentur : et interim post finem libri hoc capitulum ferebatur : quod juxta consuetudinem nostram obelo, id est veru, prænotavimus."

she may read the Prophets, the Pentateuch, the Kings and Chronicles, but *no* Apocryphal books; or, if she does, she should first, by way of caution, be informed of their true character. Jerom speaks of the fables of Bel and the Dragon, and says that the Apocryphal books do not belong to those whose names they bear, and that they contain several forgeries. In all his works, he explicitly maintains the distinction between canonical and Apocryphal books. " The latter," he says, " the church does not receive among canonical Scriptures; they may be read for edification of the people, but are not to be esteemed of authority for proving any doctrine of religion." His canon of the Old Testament was precisely that of the Jews; and though he and other ancient Christian writers sometimes quote the Apocryphal books, by way of illustration, as they also do Heathen writings, yet they had a supreme regard for the Jewish canon, consisting of those books which were received by the Jewish people as sacred and divine.

Epiphanius, Bishop of Constantia, in the island of Cyprus, who wrote in the year 392, has thrice enumerated the books of the Old Testament as held by the Jews. Of the Apocryphal books he makes no mention, except of the Wisdom of Solomon, and the Wisdom of Jesus the son of Sirach, of which, after referring to the canonical books, he says, " They likewise are useful, but not brought into the same number with the foregoing, and, therefore, are not placed in the ark of the covenant."

Rufinus, presbyter of Aquileia, who wrote about

the year 397, after giving distinct catalogues of the sacred Scriptures, both of the Old Testament and the New, adds as follows: "However, it ought to be observed, that there are also other books that are not canonical, but have been called by our forefathers ecclesiastical, as the Wisdom of Solomon, and another which is called the Wisdom of the Son of Sirach; and among the Latins, is called by the general name of Ecclesiasticus; by which title is denoted, not the author of the books, but the quality of the writing. In the same rank is the book of Tobit, and Judith, and the books of the Maccabees. In the New Testament is the book of the Shepherd, or of Hermas, which is called the Two Ways, or the Judgment of Peter. All which they would have to be read in the churches, but not to be alleged by way of authority for proving articles of faith. Other Scriptures they call Apocryphal, which they would not have to be read in the churches." Thus it appears, that all the early Christian writers, while they were unanimous in acknowledging the Jewish Scriptures, rejected, with one accord, the Apocryphal books as uncanonical, or destitute of all claim to inspiration.

The first catalogue of the books of the Old Testament, in which Apocryphal books were added to the Jewish canon, although some refer it to a later date, is that of the third, sometimes called the sixth council of Carthage, which assembled in the year 397, when the books of the Maccabees were reckoned in the number of canonical books. But the word canonical appears to have been used by them loosely, as comprehending not only the Jewish Scriptures, which were admitted as the rule of faith, but those Apocryphal books also, which they esteemed to be useful. It is said, too, that Innocent, Bishop of Rome, in the year 402, confirmed this catalogue; but this is doubtful. Other fathers and councils, in the succeeding centuries, speak occasionally of these books as canonical, meaning, however, as appears, in the secondary sense, and generally with express declarations of their inferiority to the Jewish canon, when that question was agitated. But at length the Council of Trent, in the sixteenth century, in order to check the progress of the Reformation, pronounced the Apocryphal books (except the prayer of Manasseh, and the third and fourth books of Esdras) to be strictly canonical. From that period they have usurped the name of inspired Scriptures, and have been intermingled with the canonical books in the Bibles of Roman Catholics. Thus, in direct opposition to the command of God, an addition was made to the sacred canon, in the very worst form, of many entire books, and these not corresponding with the inspired writings, but in numerous instances, and most important particulars, directly contradicting them.*

---

* The following list of books, which is annexed to the decree of the Council of Trent, will show how completely the Apocryphal books are intermingled in Roman Catholic Bibles. The

We have thus observed the manner in which the Apocryphal books came to be connected with the canonical Scriptures. They were not admitted into the canon without much opposition. The most distinguished Christian writers often protested against them, and although those who patronised them maintained that they never meant to dignify these writings with any authority as rules of faith, yet a presentiment, or foresight, of the abuse that might be made of them, induced many in the churches, and even whole churches, to resist their introduction. The Christian assemblies of the East were their

---

books of the New Testament are the same as in the Protestant canon.

5 of Moses, i.e.	Rest of Esther	12 Prophets the less,
Genesis	Job	i.e.
Exodus	David's Psalms, 150	Hosea
Leviticus	Proverbs	Joel
Numbers	Ecclesiastes	Amos
Deuteronomy	Song of Songs	Obadiah
Joshua	Wisdom	Jonah
Judges	Ecclesiasticus	Micah
Ruth	Isaiah	Nahum
Kings, 4	Jeremiah	Habakkuk
Chronicles, 2	Baruch	Zephaniah
Ezra, 1 and 2	Ezekiel	Haggai
Nehemiah	Daniel	Zechariah
Tobias	Song of Three Children	Malachi
Judith	Susanna	Maccabees, 2, I. & II.
Esther	Bel and the Dragon	

Four books, it will be observed, are incorporated in the body of the inspired texts of Esther and Daniel.

principal opponents, and more strictly observed the directions of the Apostle John, who had passed a great part of his life among them. This appears evidently from the conduct and decisions of the Council of Laodicea above quoted, which was held in the fourth century, and which prohibited the reading of any but the canonical books in the churches.

The introduction of the Apocryphal books probably originated in their being written, as is supposed, by Jews, who constantly refer to the authenticated history of their nation, and to the law delivered to their fathers. Although totally devoid of both external and internal evidence of their being from God, yet they came, as we have seen, to be considered as related to the Scriptures, not, indeed, as possessing Divine authority, but as profitable for instruction; and in this light they continued to be viewed till the Reformation, which was produced by an open appeal to the Word of God. In vain did the Man of Sin, at that era, protest against tampering with the long established authority of the church—in vain did he endeavour to prevent the translation and circulation of the Scriptures; the palpable abuses in the Popish system convinced multitudes that it could not be of God, and the desire of examining the Scriptures became irresistible. Amidst all this enquiry, however, the ignorance of Europe was so great, that the Council of Trent, above referred to, ventured to decree that the Apocryphal books were equal in point of authority, and were henceforth to be viewed as an integral part of the Word of God, and to pronounce its anathema on all who should reject them.

It was then that the design of Satan, in bringing about the unhallowed connexion between the Holy Scriptures and the Apocryphal writings, was brought to light. He had patiently waited his opportunity, and, satisfied with having the books of lying prophets placed in juxtaposition with the Word of God, had not prosecuted the advantage which he had obtained; but he well knew, that, in the course of events, this undefined association of truth and error—of sacred and profane—would increase to more ungodliness; and when the throne of Antichrist seemed tottering to its foundation, he successfully propped it up by the adulteration of the Word of God, for which the unfaithfulness of Christians for a thousand years had paved the way. While the reformers strenuously denied the authority of the Apocrypha, and loudly protested against the blasphemous decree by which it was sanctioned as Divine, they yielded to the suggestions of a sinful expediency, and allowed it to retain that affinity to the Scriptures which it had long possessed, by being translated, bound up, and circulated along with them. And who can tell how far this has tended to produce that denial of the full inspiration of the Scriptures, which is so lamentably common among Protestants? Be this as it may, the book of God is to the present hour very generally profaned by this unhallowed connexion, more or less defined or acknowledged. But God now appears to have arisen to plead the cause of his own Word. The question in regard to the Apocrypha has, in the course of his adorable providence, begun to be agitated, and it will issue in the purification of the fountain from which those waters flow, that are destined to diffuse life and felicity over the world. Ezek. xlvii. 8, 9. The means by which the attention of Christians has been directed to this all-important subject are very remarkable, and we are forcibly reminded, that, in the good providence of God, the most important effects frequently proceed from causes which at first appear to have a directly opposite tendency, and that the friends of truth have often reason to rejoice in the issue of events which at first occasioned the greatest alarm. We are thus taught to adore Him who makes the wrath of man to praise him, and causes human folly and wickedness to redound to the praise of his own glory.

On the subject of adding the Apocryphal writings to the Holy Scriptures, Bishop Hall expresses himself in the following terms: " The Scripture complains justly of three main wrongs offered to it. The first, of addition to the canon. Who can endure a piece of new cloth to be patched unto an old garment? or, what can follow hence, but that the rent should be worse? Who can abide, that, against the faithful information of the Hebrews; against the clear testimonies of Melito, Cyril, Athanasius, Origen, Hilary, Jerom, Rufinus, Nazianzen; against their own doctors, both of the middle and latest age; six whole books should, by their fatherhoods of Trent, be, under pain of a curse, imperiously obtruded upon God and his church? Whereof yet, some purpose to their readers no better than magical jugglings; others, bloody self-murders; others, lying fables; and others, Heathenish rites; not without a public applause in the relation.... *We know full well how great impiety it is, to fasten upon the God of Heaven the weak conceptions of a human wit:* neither can we be any whit moved with the idle crack of the Tridentine curse, while we hear God thundering in our ears, 'If any man add unto these words, God shall add unto him the plagues written in this book;' (Apocal. xxii. 18.) Neither know I, whether it be more *wickedly audacious to fasten on God those things which he never wrote;* or to weaken the authority, and deny the sufficiency, of what he hath written."

While there are those who have dared to add certain Apocryphal books to the Jewish canon, which form no part of it, but are the production of lying prophets, and therefore subjected to the curse pronounced upon such by God, there are others who have contended that certain books included in that canon do not constitute a part of Divine revelation. This has been particularly the case respecting the book of Esther and the Song of Solomon, which, it has been alleged, are not quoted in the New Testament. But though this may be true as to particular passages, yet the books themselves are quoted each time that either the Lord Jesus Christ or his Apostles refer to what " is written," or to " the Scriptures," of which they form a part. Exceptions have been made to these books from their contents, and on this ground their claim to be canonical has been doubted. Such a sentiment is the effect of inconsiderate rashness and presumption. The arrogant wisdom of man may now pretend to quarrel with the Book of Esther for not containing the name of God, and to find impurity in the Song of Solomon, or imperfection in other books of Holy Writ. But the authority of Jesus Christ has given a sanction to every book in the Jewish canon, and blasphemy is written on the forehead of that theory that alleges imperfection, error, or sin, in any book in that sacred collection. It is not necessary to urge, that the genuineness and authenticity of the two books referred to were not only not doubted, but that they were received by the Jews with peculiar veneration, which is a well-known fact. The incontrovertible proof respecting their authenticity and inspiration is, that *they form a part of those Scriptures which were committed to the Jewish Church, and sanctioned by the Lord and his Apostles*. On these incontrovertible grounds, all the books of the Old Testament Scriptures are most surely believed by the great body of Christians to be the oracles of God; and could it be shown that any one of them is not worthy of being received as a part of the sacred canon, this would invalidate the claim of all the rest. That man, therefore, who rejects a single one of these books as not being canonical, in other words, equally the dictates of inspiration as the rest, proves that he does not rely on the true and secure foundation which God has laid for entire confidence in that portion of the faithful record of his Word. He does it in defiance of all the foregoing evidence; and to deny the whole volume of inspiration would not require the adoption of any other principle than that on which he is proceeding.

NEW TESTAMENT.

From the time when the Old Testament was completed by Malachi, the last of the prophets, till the publication of the New, about 460 years elapsed. During the life of Jesus Christ, and for some time after his ascension, nothing on the subject of his mission was committed to writing. The period of his remaining on earth, may be regarded as an intermediate state between the Old and the New Dispensation. His personal ministry was confined to the land of Judea; and, by means of his miracles and discourses, together with those of his disciples, the attention of men, in that country, was sufficiently directed to his doctrine. They were also in possession of the Old Testament Scriptures, which, at that season, it was of the greatest importance they should consult, in order to compare the ancient predictions with what was then taking place. Immediately after the resurrection of Jesus Christ, his disciples, in the most public manner, and in the place where he had been crucified, proclaimed that event, and the whole of the doctrine which he had commanded them to preach. In this service they continued personally to labour for a considerable time, first among their countrymen the Jews, and afterwards among the other nations. During the period between the resurrection and the publication of the New Testament, the churches possessed miraculous gifts, and the prophets were enabled to explain the predictions of the Old Testament, and to point out their fulfilment.

After their doctrine had every where attracted attention, and, in spite of the most violent opposition, had forced its way through the civilized world; and when churches, or societies of Christians, were collected, not only in Judea, but in the most celebrated cities of Italy, Greece, and Asia Minor, the Scriptures of the New Testament were written by the Apostles and other inspired men, and intrusted to the keeping of these churches.

The whole of the New Testament was not written at once, but in different parts, and on various occasions. Six of the Apostles, and two inspired disciples who accompanied them in their journeys, were employed in this work. The histories which it contains of the life of Christ, known by the name of the Gospels, were composed by four of his contemporaries, two of whom had been constant attendants on his public ministry. The first of these was published within a few years* after his death, in that very country where he had lived, and among the people who had seen him and observed his conduct. The history called the "Acts of the Apostles," which

---

* " Some have thought that it was written no more than eight years after our Lord's ascension; others have reckoned it no fewer than fifteen."—*Campbell's Preface to Matthew's Gospel.*

contains an account of their proceedings, and of the progress of the Gospel, from Jerusalem, among the Gentile nations, was published about the year 64, being 30 years after our Lord's crucifixion, by one who, although not an Apostle, declares that he had " perfect understanding of all things from the very first," and who had written one of the Gospels. This book, commencing with a detail of proceedings, from the resurrection of Jesus Christ, carries down the evangelical history till the arrival of Paul as a prisoner at Rome. The Epistles, addressed to churches in particular places, to believers scattered up and down in different countries, or to individuals, in all twenty-one in number, were separately written by five of the Apostles, from seventeen to twenty, thirty, and thirty-five years after the death of Christ. Four of these writers had accompanied the Lord Jesus during his life, and had been " eyewitnesses of his majesty." The fifth was the Apostle Paul, who, as he expresses it, was " one born out of due time," but who had likewise seen Jesus Christ, and had been empowered by him to work miracles, which were " the signs of an apostle." One of these five also wrote the book of Revelation, about the year ninety-six, addressed to the seven churches in Asia, containing epistles to these churches from Jesus Christ himself, with various instructions for the immediate use of all Christians, together with a prophetical view of the kingdom of God till the end of time. These several pieces, which compose the Scriptures of the New Testament, were received by the churches with the highest veneration; and, as the instructions they contain, though partially addressed, were equally intended for all, they were immediately copied, and handed about from one church to another, till each was in possession of the whole. The volume of the New Testament was thus completed before the death of the last of the Apostles, most of whom had sealed their testimony with their blood.

From the manner in which these Scriptures were at first circulated, some of their parts were necessarily longer of reaching certain places than others. These, of course, could not be so soon received into the canon as the rest. Owing to this circumstance, and to that of a few of the books being addressed to individual believers, or to their not having the name of their writers affixed, or the designation of Apostle added, a doubt for a time existed among some respecting the genuineness of the Epistle to the Hebrews, the Epistle of James, the 2d Epistle of Peter, the 2d and 3d Epistles of John, the Epistle of Jude, and the Book of Revelation. These, however, though not universally, were generally acknowledged; while all the other books of the New Testament were without dispute received from the beginning. This discrimination proves the scrupulous care of the first churches on this highly important subject.

At length these books, which had not been admitted at first, were, like the rest, universally received, not by the votes of a council, as is sometimes asserted, but after deliberate and free enquiry by many separate churches, under the superintending providence of God, in different parts of the world.

It is at the same time a certain fact, that no other books besides those which at present compose the volume of the New Testament, were admitted by the churches. Several Apocryphal writings were published under the name of Jesus Christ and his Apostles, which are mentioned by the writers of the four first centuries, most of which have perished, though some are still extant. Few or none of them were composed before the second century, and several of them were forged so late as the third century. But they were not acknowledged as authentic by the first Christians, and were rejected, by those who have noticed them, as spurious and heretical.* Histories, too, as might have been expected, were written of the life of Christ, and one forgery was attempted, of a letter said to be written by Jesus Christ himself to Abgarus, King of Edessa; but of the first, none were received as of any authority, and the last was universally rejected. " Besides our Gospels, and the Acts of the Apostles," says Paley,

---

* " These forged writings," says Lardner, " do not oppose, but confirm, the account given us in the canonical Scriptures. They all take for granted the dignity of our Lord's person, and his power of working miracles; they acknowledge the certainty of there having been such persons as Matthew and the other Evangelists, and Peter and the other Apostles. They authenticate the general and leading facts contained in the New Testament. They presuppose that the Apostles received from Christ a commission to propagate his religion, and a supernatural power to enforce its authority. And thus they indirectly establish the truth and divine original of the Gospel."

" no Christian history, claiming to be written by an apostle, or apostolical man, is quoted within 300 years after the birth of Christ, by any writer now extant or known ; or, if quoted, is quoted with marks of censure and rejection."

This agreement of Christians respecting the Scriptures, when we consider their many differences in other respects, is the more remarkable, since it took place without any public authority being interposed. " We have no knowledge," says the above author, " of any interference of authority in the question before the council of Laodicea, in the year 363. Probably the decree of this council rather declared than regulated the public judgment, or, more properly speaking, the judgment of some neighbouring churches—the council itself consisting of no more than thirty or forty bishops of Lydia and the adjoining countries. Nor does its authority seem to have extended farther.' But the fact, that no public authority was interposed, does not require to be supported by the above reasoning. The churches at the beginning, being separated from each other in distant countries, necessarily judged for themselves in this matter, and the decree of the council was founded on the coincidence of their judgment.

In delivering this part of his written revelation, God proceeded as he had formerly done in the publication of the Old Testament Scriptures. For a considerable time, his will was declared to mankind through the medium of oral tradition. At length he saw meet, in his wisdom, to give it a more permanent form. But this did not take place, till a people, separated from all others, was provided for its reception. In the same manner, when Jesus Christ set up his kingdom in the world, of which the nation of Israel was a type, he first made known his will by means of verbal communication, through his servants whom he commissioned and sent out for that purpose; and when, through their means, he had prepared his subjects and collected them into churches, to be the depositaries of his Word, he caused it to be delivered to them in writing. His kingdom was not to consist of any particular nation, like that of Israel, but of all those individuals, in every part of the world, who should believe in his name. It was to be ruled, not by means of human authority, or compulsion of any kind, but solely by his authority. These sacred writings were thus intrusted to a people prepared for their reception— a nation among the nations, but singularly distinct from all the rest, who guarded and preserved them with the same inviolable attachment as the Old Testament Scriptures had experienced from the Jews.

Respecting the lateness of the time when the Scriptures of the New Testament were written, no objection can be offered, since they were published before that generation passed which had witnessed the transactions they record. The dates of these writings fall within the period of the lives of many who were in full manhood when the Lord Jesus Christ was upon earth; and the facts detailed in the histories, and referred to in the Epistles, being of the most public nature, were still open to full investigation. It must also be recollected, that the

Apostles and disciples, during the whole intermediate period, were publicly proclaiming to the world the same things that were afterwards recorded in their writings.

Had these Scriptures been published before associations of Christians were in existence, to whose care could they have been intrusted? What security would there have been for their preservation, or that they would not have been corrupted? In the way that was adopted, they were committed to faithful men, who, viewing them as the charter of their own salvation, and the doctrine which they contained as the appointed means of rescuing their fellow creatures from misery and guilt, watched over their preservation with the most zealous and assiduous care.

But unless the whole manner of communicating the revelation of God, in these Scriptures, had been altered, it is not possible, that, excepting the accounts of the life of Jesus Christ, they could have been earlier committed to writing. The history of the Acts of the Apostles, being carried down to about the year 63 of the Christian era, could not, it is evident, have been published sooner. The Epistles are not addressed to men of the world, or to the whole inhabitants of particular countries, but exclusively to believers. The truth conveyed in them is not delivered in an abstract form, but in the way of immediate application to existing cases and circumstances. This practical method of communicating the doctrine, and of recording the laws, of the kingdom of Christ, which commends itself to every reflecting mind, could not, it is manifest, have been adopted till societies of Christians were in existence, and till they had existed for some considerable time. In this way, too, we have an undeniable proof of the success of the Apostles in the rapid progress of the Gospel. We are made acquainted, as we could not otherwise have been, with their zeal, resolution, self-denial, disinterestedness, patience, and meekness, and have the most convincing evidence of the extraordinary gifts they possessed. We are also put in possession of indubitable evidence of the miraculous gifts conferred on the first Christians, as well as of their sincerity, courage, and patience.

Thus were the Scriptures, as we now possess them, delivered to the first churches. By the concurrent testimony of all antiquity, both of friends and foes, they were received by Christians of different sects, and were constantly appealed to on all hands, in the controversies that arose among them. Commentaries upon them were written at a very early period, and translations made into different languages. Formal catalogues of them were published, and they were attacked by the adversaries of Christianity, who not only did not question, but expressly admitted, the facts they contained, and that they were the genuine productions of the persons whose names they bore.

In this manner the Scriptures were also secured from the danger of being in any respect altered or vitiated. " The books of Scripture," says Augustine, " could not have been corrupted. If such an attempt had been made by any one, his design would have been prevented and defeated. His alterations would have been immediately detected by many and more ancient copies. The difficulty of succeeding in such an attempt is apparent hence, that the Scriptures were early translated into divers languages, and copies of them were numerous. The alterations which any one attempted to make would have been soon perceived ; just even as now, in fact, lesser faults in some copies are amended by comparing ancient copies or those of the original. . . . If any one," continues Augustine, " should charge you with having interpolated some texts alleged by you as favourable to your cause, what would you say ? Would you not immediately answer that it is impossible for you to do such a thing in books read by all Christians ? And that if any such attempt had been made by you, it would have been presently discerned and defeated by comparing the ancient copies ? Well, then, for the same reason that the Scriptures cannot be corrupted by you, neither could they be corrupted by any other people."

Accordingly, the uniformity of the manuscripts of the Holy Scriptures that are extant, which are incomparably more numerous than those of any ancient author, and which are dispersed through so many countries, and in so great a variety of languages, is truly astonishing. It demonstrates both the veneration in which the Scriptures have always been held, and the singular care that has been taken in transcribing them. The number of various readings, that by the most minute and laborious investigation and collations of manuscripts have been discovered in them, said to amount to one hundred and fifty thousand, though at first sight they may seem calculated to diminish confidence in the sacred text, yet in no degree whatever do they affect its credit and integrity. They consist almost wholly in palpable errors in transcription, grammatical and verbal differences, such as the insertion or omission of a letter or article, the substitution of a word for its equivalent, the transposition of a word or two in a sentence. Taken altogether, they neither change nor affect a single doctrine or duty announced or enjoined in the Word of God.* When, therefore, we consider the great antiquity of the sacred books, the almost infinite number of copies, of versions, of editions, which have been made of them in all languages—in languages which have not any analogy one with another, among nations differing so much in their customs and their religious opinions;—when we reflect on these things, it is truly astonishing, and can only be ascribed to the watchful providence of God over his own Word, that amongst the various readings, nothing truly essential can be discerned, which relates to either precept or doctrine, or which breaks that connexion, that unity, which subsists in all the various parts of Divine revelation, and which demonstrates the whole to be the work of one and the same Spirit.

---

* Dr Kennicott examined and collated 600 Hebrew manuscripts, and so trifling were the variations he discovered, that it has been objected, though very unjustly, that he had effected nothing by all his labours.

In proof that the Scriptures were published and delivered to the churches in the age to which their dates refer, we have the attestation of a connected chain of Christian writers, from that period to the present day. No fewer than six of these authors, part of whose works are still extant, were contemporaries of the Apostles.

BARNABAS was the companion of the Apostle Paul. He is the author of an Epistle, which was well known among the early Christians. It is still extant, and refers to the Apostolic writings.

CLEMENT was the third bishop of the church at Rome, and is mentioned by Paul in his Epistle to the Philippians. He has left a long Epistle, which is extant, though not entire, written in name of the church at Rome to the church at Corinth, in which the latter is admonished to adhere to the commands of Christ. Irenæus says that it was written by Clement, "who had seen the blessed Apostles, and conversed with them; who had the preaching of the Apostles still sounding in his ears, and their traditions before his eyes. Nor he alone, for there were then still many alive, who had been taught by the Apostles. In the time, therefore, of this Clement, when there was no small dissension among the brethren at Corinth, the church at Rome sent a most excellent letter to the Corinthians, persuading them to peace among themselves." About 80 or 90 years after this letter was written, Dionysius, the Bishop at Corinth, declares, that "it had been wont to be read in that church from ancient times." It contains several quotations from the New Testament Scriptures, and allusions to them.

HERMAS also, contemporary with the Apostles, has left a book that still remains, called, " The Shepherd of Hermas," in which he quotes and enforces the doctrine of Scripture.

IGNATIUS was bishop of the church at Antioch, about 37 years after Christ's ascension. He suffered martyrdom at Rome under the Emperor Trajan. Ignatius has left several Epistles that are still extant, which give testimony to Jesus Christ and his doctrine. He declares, that he " fled to the Gospels as the flesh of Jesus, and to the Apostles as the elders of the church."

POLYCARP had been taught by the Apostles, and had conversed with many who had seen Christ. He was appointed by the Apostles, Bishop of the church at Smyrna. One epistle of his still remains, which evinces the respect that he and other Christians bore for the Scriptures. Irenæus, who, in his youth, had been a disciple of Polycarp, says, concerning him, in a letter to Florinus,—" I saw you when I was very young, in the Lower Asia with Polycarp. For I better remember the affairs of that time, than those which have lately happened; the things which we learn in our childhood growing up with the soul, and uniting themselves to it. Insomuch that I can tell the place in which the blessed Polycarp sat and taught, and his going out and coming in, and the manner of his life, and the form of his person, and the discourses he made to the people; and how he related his conversation with John, and others who had seen the Lord, and how he related their sayings, and what he had heard from them concerning the Lord; both concerning his miracles and his doctrine, as he had received them from the eyewitnesses of the Word of Life; all which Polycarp related agreeable to the Scriptures. These things I then, through the mercy of God toward me, diligently heard and attended to, recording them not on paper, but upon my heart. And through the grace of God I continually renew the remembrance of them." Polycarp was condemned to the flames at Smyrna, the proconsul being present, and all the people in the amphitheatre demanding his death. Thus, like Ignatius, he confirmed his testimony to the Scriptures with his blood.

Papias was a hearer of the Apostle John, and a companion of Polycarp. He was the author of five books, which are now lost, but which, according to quotations from them that remain, bore testimony to the Scriptures. He expressly ascribes their respective Gospels to Matthew and Mark.

The above six writers had all lived and conversed with some of the Apostles. Those parts which remain of the writings of the first five, who are called the Apostolical Fathers, are valuable on account of their antiquity; and all of them contain some important testimony to the Scriptures.

About twenty years after these writers follows Justin Martyr. He was born about the year 89, and suffered martyrdom about the year 163. Originally he had been a Heathen philosopher; and, in his dialogue with Trypho the Jew, he relates the circumstances of his conversion to Christianity. From his works might be extracted almost a complete life of Christ; and he uniformly represents the Scriptures as containing the authentic account of his doctrine. The Gospels, he says, were read and expounded every Sunday in the solemn assemblies of the Christians. He particularly mentions the Acts of the Apostles, along with the books of the Old Testament, which were also regularly read as in the Jewish synagogues; and he appeals to the Scriptures as writings open to all the world, and read by Jews and Gentiles. He presented two apologies for the Christian religion; the first to the Emperor Antoninus Pius, in the year 140; the second to Marcus Antoninus, the philosopher, in the year 162. Both these apologies are still extant; the first entire, of the second the beginning is wanting.

DIONYSIUS, TATIAN, and HEGESIPPUS, wrote about thirty years after Justin Martyr, and give their testimony to the Scriptures. Hegesippus relates, that, travelling from Palestine to Rome, he visited in his journey many bishops; and that " in every succession, and in every city, the same doctrine is taught which the law and the prophets and the Lord teacheth."

About the year 177, the churches of Lyons and Vienne in France sent a relation of the persecutions they suffered to the churches in Asia and Phrygia. POTHINUS, bishop of the church at Lyons, was then 90 years old; and in his early life was contemporary with the Apostle John. This letter, which is preserved entire, makes exact references to the Scriptures.

Irenæus succeeded Pothinus as bishop at Lyons. In his youth, as has already been noticed, he had been a disciple of Polycarp, who was a disciple of the Apostle John. Thus he was only one step removed from the Apostles. Irenæus gives a most ample testimony, both to the genuineness and the authenticity of the Scriptures. " We have not received," says he, " the knowledge of the way of our salvation by any others than those by whom the Gospel has been brought to us; which Gospel they first preached, and afterwards, by the will of God, committed to writing, that it might be for time to come the foundation and pillar of our faith.—For after that our Lord rose from the dead, and they (the Apostles) were endued from above with the power of the Holy Ghost coming down upon them, they received a perfect knowledge of all things. They then went forth to all the ends of the earth, declaring to men the blessing of heavenly peace, having, all of them, and every one alike, the Gospel of God. Matthew, then among the Jews, wrote a Gospel in their own language, while Peter and Paul were preaching the Gospel at Rome, and founding a church there. And after their exit, (death or departure,) Mark also, the disciple and interpreter of Peter, delivered to us in writing the things that had been preached by Peter; and Luke, the companion of Paul, put down in a book the Gospel preached by him (Paul.) Afterwards John, the disciple of the Lord, who also leaned upon his breast, he likewise published a Gospel while he dwelt at Ephesus in Asia. And all these have delivered to us, that there is one God, the maker of the heaven and the earth, declared by the law and the prophets, and one Christ, the Son of God. And he who does not assent to them, despiseth indeed those who knew the mind of the Lord: but he despiseth also Christ himself the Lord, and he despiseth likewise the Father, and is self-condemned, resisting and opposing his own salvation, as all heretics do."—" The tradition of the Apostles hath spread itself over the whole universe; and all they who search after the sources of truth, will find this tradition to be held sacred in every church. We might enumerate all those who have been appointed bishops to those churches by the Apostles, and all their successors up to our days. It is by this uninterrupted succession that we have received the tradition which actually exists in the church, and also the doctrine of truth as it is preached by the Apostles."

After giving some reasons why he supposed the number of the Gospels was precisely four, Irenæus says, "Whence it is manifest that the Word, the Former of all things, who sits upon the cherubim, and upholds all things, having appeared to men, has given to us a Gospel of a fourfold character, but joined in one spirit.—The Gospel according to John discloses his primary and glorious generation from the Father: 'In the beginning was the Word.'— But the Gospel according to Luke, being of a priestly character, begins with Zacharias the priest offering incense to God.—Matthew relates his generation, which is according to men: 'The book of the generation of Jesus Christ, the son of David, the son of Abraham.'—Mark begins from the prophetic spirit which came down from above to men, saying, 'The beginning of the Gospel of Jesus Christ, as it is written in Esaias the prophet.'"

The above passage distinctly ascertains, that the four Gospels, as we have them, and no more, were equally received and acknowledged by the first churches.

Irenæus farther says, "The Gospel according to Matthew was written to the Jews, for they earnestly desired a Messiah of the seed of David, and Matthew, having also the same desire to a yet greater degree, strove by all means to give them full satisfaction that Christ was of the seed of David, wherefore he began with his genealogy."—"Wherefore also Mark, the interpreter and follower of Peter, makes this the beginning of his evangelic writing, 'The beginning of the Gospel of Jesus Christ, the Son of God.' And in the end of the Gospel, Mark says, 'So then, the Lord Jesus, after he had spoken to them, was received up into Heaven, and sat on the right hand of God.'"—"But if any one rejects Luke, as if he did not know the truth, he will be convicted of throwing away the Gospel, of which he professeth to be a disciple. For there are many, and those very necessary, parts of the Gospel, which we know by his means." He then refers to several particulars, which are known only from Luke.

The Acts of the Apostles is a book much quoted by Irenæus, as written by Luke, the companion of the Apostles. There are few things recorded in that book which have not been mentioned by him. " And that Luke," says he, " was inseparable from Paul, and his fellow-worker in the Gospel, he himself shows, not boasting of it indeed, but obliged to it for the sake of truth."

Irenæus quotes largely from the Epistles of Paul, and remarks, that this Apostle " frequently uses hyperbata," (or transpositions of words from their natural order,) " because of the rapidity of his words, and because of the mighty force of 'the Spirit in him.'" The book of Revelation Irenæus often quotes, and says, " It was seen no long time ago, but almost in our own age, at the end of the reign of Domitian." He mentions the code of the Old Testament and of the New, and calls the one, as well as the other, the Oracles of God.

Speaking of the Scriptures in general, he says, " well knowing that the Scriptures are perfect, as being dictated by the Word of God and his Spirit."— " A heavy punishment awaits those who add to or take from the Scriptures."—" But we, following the one and the only true God as our teacher, and having his words as a rule of truth, do always speak the same things concerning the same things."

ATHENAGORAS, MILTIADES, THEOPHILUS, and PANTÆNUS, who lived at the same time with Irenæus, all bear testimony to the Scriptures. Some of their works remain, and others are lost.

CLEMENT, of Alexandria, followed Irenæus at the distance of sixteen years. He was a man of great learning, and presided in the Catechetical School at

Alexandria. Clement travelled into different countries in search of information. " The law and the prophets, together with the Gospels," he says, " conduct to one and the same knowledge in the name of Christ."—" One God and Almighty Lord is taught by the law and the prophets, and the blessed Gospels." He has given a distinct account of the order in which the four Gospels were written. The Gospels which contain the genealogies, were, he says, written first, Mark's next, and John's the last. He repeatedly quotes the four Gospels by the names of their authors, and expressly ascribes the Acts of the Apostles to Luke. His quotations from the Scriptures of the New Testament are numerous, and he calls them "the Scriptures of the Lord," and the " true evangelical canon."

Next to Clement, and in the same age, comes TERTULLIAN, who was born at Carthage about the year 160. He was a man of extensive learning, and the most considerable of all the Latin writers on Christianity. He wrote a very valuable apology for the Christians, about the year 198, addressed to the governors of provinces, which is still extant. He gives the most ample attestation to the Scriptures, quoting them so frequently, that, as Lardner observes, there are more and longer quotations of the small volume of the New Testament in this one Christian author, than there are of all the works of Cicero in writers of all characters for several ages. After enumerating many churches which had been gathered by Paul and the other Apostles, he declares, that not those churches only which were called Apostolical, but all who have fellowship with them in the same faith, received the four Gospels, and that these had been in the possession of the churches from the beginning. He also affirms, that the original manuscripts of the Apostles, at least some of them, had been preserved till the age in which he lived, and were then to be seen.

"In the first place," says Tertullian, "we lay this down for a certain truth, that the Evangelic Scriptures have for their authors the Apostles, to whom the work of publishing the Gospel was committed by the Lord himself; and also Apostolical men.—Among the Apostles, John and Matthew teach us the faith; among Apostolical men, Luke and Mark refresh it, going upon the same principles as concerning the one God the Creator, and his Christ born of a virgin, the accomplishment of the law and the prophets.—If it be certain that that is most genuine which is most ancient, that most ancient which is from the beginning, and that from the beginning which is from the Apostles; in like manner, it will be also certain that that has been delivered from the Apostles which is held sacred in the churches of the Apostles. Let us then see what milk the Corinthians received from Paul, to what rule the Galatians were reduced, what the Philippians read, what the Thessalonians, the Ephesians, and also the Romans recite, who are near to us; with whom both Peter and Paul left the Gospel sealed with their blood. We have also churches which are the disciples of John; for, though Marcion rejects his Revelation, the succession of Bishops, traced up to the beginning, will show it to have John for its author. We know also the original of other churches, (that is, that they are Apostolical.) I say, then, that with them, but not with them only that are Apostolical, but with all who have fellowship with them in the same faith, is that Gospel of Luke received, which we so zealously maintain. That is the genuine entire Gospel of Luke, not that which had been curtailed and altered by Marcion. The same authority of the Apostolical churches will support the other Gospels, which we have from them, and according to them, (that is, according to their copies,) I mean John's and Matthew's, although that likewise which Mark published may be said to be Peter's, whose interpreter Mark was, for Luke's digest also is often ascribed to Paul." Tertullian says that Matthew's Gospel began in this manner,— " The book of the generation of Jesus Christ, the son of David, the son of Abraham." The Acts of the Apostles are often quoted by him under that title: he calls them Luke's Commentary, or History.

" I will," says Tertullian, " by no means say Gods nor Lords, but I will follow the Apostle; so that, if the Father and the Son are to be mentioned together, I will say God the Father, and Jesus Christ the Lord; but when I mention Christ only, I can call him God, as the Apostle does." *" Of whom Christ came, who is,"* says he, *" over all, God blessed for ever."*

To Tertullian succeeds a multitude of Christian writers. Of the works of these authors, only fragments and quotations remain, in which several testimonies to the Gospels are found. In one of them is an abstract of the whole Gospel history.

After those writers, and at the distance of twenty-five years from Tertullian, comes the celebrated Origen of Alexandria, of whom it is said, that " he did not so much recommend Christianity by what he preached, or by what he wrote, as by the general tenor of his life." He was born about 150 years after the resurrection of Jesus Christ. In the quantity of his writings he exceeded the most laborious of the Greek and Latin writers. He gives full and decisive testimony to the Scriptures. He says, " that the four Gospels alone are received without dispute by the whole church of God under heaven;" and he subjoins a history of their respective authors. " The first," says Origen, " is written by Matthew, once a publican, afterwards an Apostle of Jesus Christ. The second is that according to Mark, who wrote it as Peter dictated to him, who therefore calls him his son in his Catholic Epistle. The third is that according to Luke, the Gospel commended by Paul, published for the sake of the Gentile converts. Lastly, that according to John." He speaks of the Acts of the Apostles as an uncontested book, and gives the same account concerning Mark's Gospel as having been written under the direction of the Apostle Peter, which is given by Clement. It is reckoned a monument of the humility of Peter, that several very remarkable circumstances in his favour, that are related by the other Evangelists, are not mentioned, or even hinted at, by Mark.

Origen uniformly quotes the Epistle to the Hebrews as the writing of the Apostle Paul, and the Book of Revelation as the writing of the Apostle

John. His quotations of Scripture are so numerous, that Dr Mill says, " if we had all his works remaining, we should have before us almost the whole text of the Bible. He expresses, in the most unqualified terms, his opinion of the authority of the books of the New Testament as inspired writings, and says, that " the sacred books are not writings of men, but have been written and delivered to us from the inspiration of the Holy Spirit, by the will of the Father of all, through Jesus Christ." He urges, with earnestness, the reading of the Old and New Testament Scriptures, as a sacred obligation in the churches of Christ. " Food," says he, " is eaten, physic is taken; though the good effect is not presently perceived, a benefit is expected in time, and may be obtained. So it is with the Holy Scriptures; though, at the very time of reading of them, there be no sensible advantage, yet, in the end, they will be thought profitable for strengthening virtuous dispositions, and weakening the habits of vice.—The true food of the rational nature is the Word of God.—Let us come daily to the wells of the Scriptures, the waters of the Holy Spirit, and there draw and carry thence a full vessel. The greatest torment of demons is to see men reading the Word of God, and labouring to understand the Divine law."

In his Apology for the Christian Religion, in answer to Celsus the Epicurean philosopher, Origen, when giving a quotation from Scripture, says that it is written, " not in any private book, or such as are read by a few persons only, but in books read by every body." In that Apology, he has preserved, from the writings of Celsus, most distinct and complete attestations to the Gospel history.

Gregory, Bishop of Neocesaria, and Dionysius of Alexandria, scholars of Origen, and the well-known Cyprian, Bishop at Carthage, come about twenty years after Origen. Their writings abound with copious citations from the Scriptures, to which they give their full and particular attestation. Cyprian says, " The church is watered, like Paradise, by four rivers, that is, four Gospels."

Within forty years after Cyprian, Victorinus, Bishop at Pettaw, in Germany, and a multitude of Christian writers, all testify their profound respect for the Scriptures.

About the year 306, Arnobius and Lactantius wrote in support of the Christian religion. Lactantius argues in its defence, from the consistency, simplicity, disinterestedness, and sufferings of the writers of the Gospels. Arnobius vindicates the credit of the writers of the Gospels, observing, that they were eyewitnesses of the facts which they relate, and that their ignorance of the arts of composition was rather a confirmation of their testimony, than an objection to it.

Eusebius, Bishop at Cæsarea, born about the year 270, wrote about fifteen years after the above authors. He composed a History of Christianity, from its origin to his own time; and has handed down many valuable extracts of ancient authors, whose works have perished. In giving his testimony to the Scriptures, he shows himself to be much conversant in the works of Christian authors, and he appears to have collected every thing that had been said, before his own time, respecting the volume of the New Testament.

ATHANASIUS became bishop at Alexandria about the year 326. He expressly affirms that every one of the books of the New Testament that we now receive, are inspired Scriptures, which he specifies in their order, and ascribes them to the writers whose names they bear. He speaks of them as being constantly and publicly read in the Christian churches. Athanasius had full access to every source of information, and applied himself to ascertain the canon of the Old Testament as well as of the New. It appears, that he sent to the Emperor Constance a copy of the whole Bible, which he described as the whole inspired Scriptures. Speaking of the Scriptures, he says, " These are fountains of salvation. In them alone the doctrine of religion is taught. Let no man add to them, or take any thing from them."

It is unnecessary to carry down this chain of historical evidence any farther. The Council of Nice was called by Constantine in the year 325 ; and as Christianity had then become the established religion of the Roman empire, its history is afterwards inseparably interwoven with every thing connected with the state of the world.

From the above numerous and early writers, we have most unquestionable attestations to the integrity and authority of the Holy Scriptures. First, we have six writers who were contemporary with the Apostles, and then eleven more who lived in distant parts of the world, regularly succeeding each other during the first hundred years after the Apostles. From that period, the chain of evidence continues unbroken and uninterrupted. " When Christian advocates," says Paley, " merely tell us that we have the same reason for believing the Gospels to be written by the Evangelists whose names they bear, as we have for believing the Commentaries to be Cæsar's, the Æneid Virgil's, or the Orations Cicero's, they content themselves with an imperfect representation. They state nothing more than what is true, but they do not state the truth correctly. In the number, variety, and early date of our testimonies, we far exceed all other ancient books. For one which the most celebrated work of the most celebrated Greek or Roman writer can allege, we produce many."

The force of the above testimony is greatly strengthened by the consideration, that it is the concurring evidence of separate, independent, and well-informed writers, who lived in countries remote from one another. Clement lived at *Rome;* Ignatius, at *Antioch;* Polycarp, at *Smyrna;* Justin Martyr, in *Syria;* Irenæus, in *France;* Tertullian, at *Carthage;* Origen, in *Egypt;* Eusebius, at *Cæsarea;* Victorinus, in *Germany.* The dangers which they encountered, and the hardships and persecutions which they suffered, some of them even unto death, on account of their adherence to the Christian faith, give irresistible weight to their testimony.

" No writings," says Augustine, " ever had a better testimony afforded them than those of the Apostles and Evangelists. Nor does it weaken the credit and authority of books, received by the church of Christ from the beginning, that some other writings have been, without ground, and falsely, ascribed to the Apostles. For the like has happened, for instance, to Hippocrates; but yet his genuine works are distinguished from others which have been published under his name. We know the writings of the Apostles as we know the works of Plato, Aristotle, Cicero, Varro, and others, to be theirs, and as we know the writings of divine ecclesiastical authors; for as much as they have the testimony of contemporaries, and of those who have lived in succeeding times. I might, moreover, by way of illustration, produce for examples those now in hand. Suppose some one in time to come should deny those to be the works of Faustus, or those to be mine; how should he be satisfied but by the testimony of those of this time who knew both, and have transmitted their accounts to others? And shall not, then, the testimony of the churches, and Christian brethren, be valid here; especially when they are so numerous, and so harmonious, and the tradition is with so much ease and certainty traced down from the Apostles to our time—I say, shall any be so foolish and unreasonable as to deny or dispute the credibility of such a testimony to the Scriptures, which would be allowed in behalf of any writings whatever, whether heathen or ecclesiastical?"

In another place Augustine observes, " If you here ask us, how we know these to be the writings of the Apostles; in brief we answer, in the same way that you know the Epistles, or any other writings of Mani, to be his: for if any one should be pleased to dispute with you, and offer to deny the Epistles ascribed to Mani to be his, what would you do? Would you not laugh at the assurance of the man who denied the genuineness of writings generally allowed? As, therefore, it is certain those books are Mani's, and he would be ridiculous who should now dispute it; so certain is it that the Manichees deserve to be laughed at, or rather ought to be pitied, who dispute the truth and genuineness of those writings of the Apostles, which have been handed down as theirs from their time to this, through an uninterrupted succession of well-known witnesses."

Should it occur to any that to prove the genuineness and authenticity of the Scriptures by the testimony of the Fathers, is to sanction the traditions of the Church of Rome, they ought to consider that there is a radical distinction between these two cases. Testimony is a first principle, universally acknowledged as authoritative in its own province, as far as it is unexceptionable. The whole business of the world proceeds on this principle, and without it human affairs would run into utter confusion. That historical testimony is a legitimate source of evidence, the general sentiments of mankind admit, in the universal appeal to history for the knowledge of past events. Historical testimony may be false, but this is not peculiar to this class of first principles. We are liable to be deceived on all subjects to which our faculties are directed; but there are means by which historical evidence may be ascertained. Its proof may vary from the lowest degree of probability to the highest degree of certainty. Of many things recorded even in profane history, we can have no more doubt than we can have of truths that contain their own evidence. Now, the stress laid on the testimony of the ancient writers that have been quoted, is warranted by the most cautious laws of historical evidence; and it cannot be rejected, without entirely rejecting history as a legitimate ground of knowledge. That such writers did give such testimony, is as indisputable as any historical fact can be. And the proof of this lies open to every man who has time, opportunity, and ability to examine the subject. If so, there is no reason to reject as insufficient, in proof of the authenticity of the Bible, the same kind of evidence that is allowed to prove any other fact. But the traditions of the Church of Rome are not of this nature. They are not historical at all. They have not been written; they are nowhere to be found. It is not pretended by their friends that they possess historical evidence. They are recommended altogether on another foundation,— the authority of the church. It is said the church has had them treasured up in secret; but we can have no higher assurance of their authenticity than what we are willing to rest on the authority of the church. The difference, then, between the two cases, is manifest and essential. And clearer historical proof cannot be exhibited on any subject, than has been adduced for the genuineness and authenticity of the Holy Scriptures.

It has been supposed that if a list of the names and numbers of the books of Scripture had been recorded in any part of the canon, it would have added to our certainty respecting the Divine original of the whole. But if there were such a list, it would still remain to be decided whether the books we possess were the very books named, in words and substance, as well as in name. Indeed if the list were written, and the number of lines and words recorded, the case would still be the same. It would not in the smallest degree add to our certainty respecting their Divine original; for how could we be assured of that inspired list, but from the certainty of the book being from God that contained the list? Such a list could neither ascertain its own accuracy, nor the authenticity of the book which contained it. The authenticity of that list must have been ascertained precisely in the same manner as that of each and all of the books is now ascertained.

If, therefore, the name and number of the inspired books were contained in any epistle, it would still leave the authority of the books named, on the same foundation of the authority of the epistle in which they were named; and that authority must have been ascertained exactly in the same way by which we now ascertain the authority of each and all of the inspired books. The ultimate foundation, then, of the evidence would be the *same*, as to that particular part which contained the list; and, with respect to the books mentioned in the list, we could not be assured against their mutilation and corruption. It is quite absurd, then, to suppose that a list of the names and numbers of the inspired books would have given us better evidence of their authority. The authority of that part which contained such a list, must be ascertained in the ordinary way; and, as the stream cannot rise higher than the fountain, the authority of all the books, as resting on the testimony of one, would be no stronger than that of the one which supported them. In whatever way that one could prove its Divine authority, in the same way we now prove the authority of all.

The circumstance, then, that there is not a list of the books of inspiration contained in the page of inspiration itself, does not lessen the certainty as to the canon, nor increase the difficulty of ascertaining the truth of it. That if a list of the books of Scripture were given in the Scriptures, it would not fix the question of the canon on a surer foundation, is obvious too, from the consideration that a forgery might contain such a list, as well as an authentic document, and that the truth of such a list takes it for granted that the book which contains it is canonical. Is the second epistle of Peter put above the first, as to the certainty of its being canonical, by the assertion, " This second epistle, beloved, I now write unto you?" Does such an expression establish its being canonical? Is it not evident, on the contrary, that the epistle's being canonical must be established before the assertion, " This second epistle I now write unto you," is believed to be inspired? So far from such a list proving that the books which contain it are canonical, it is their being canonical that verifies the list. If the claim of a book of Scripture to be canonical is not ascertained, the list which it contains is not revelation. With respect to the books of the Old Testament, however, such a list is in effect given, and the inspiration of them warranted in the assertion, " All Scripture is given by inspiration." Now, the steps by which we arrive at certainty here, are few and simple. If the book of the New Testament which contains this assertion is canonical, it warrants all the books of the Old Testament which at the time of its publication were received as Scripture. We have only to enquire what books were then contained in the Jewish canon, to be assured in this matter. This is a point of testimony on which no difficulty exists. It must be observed, however, that the confidence placed in the list, or notification, rests entirely upon the authenticity of the book that contains it being previously ascertained. But if a list of the whole of the inspired books is the only thing that could ascertain with sufficient evidence such as are from God, then no man can have a thorough faith in the Scriptures, for such a list has not been given. And had it been given, it could not have secured against forgery, as has been already noticed, for nothing is easier than for a forger to give such a list. Had the Scriptures been a forgery, they would probably have recommended themselves by a very correct list.

It has been asserted that " the question of the canon is a point of erudition, not of Divine revelation." This is to undermine both the certainty and the importance of the sacred canon. The assertion, that the question of the canon is *not a point of revelation*, is false. It is not true either of the Old Testament, or of the New. The integrity of the canon of the Old Testament, is a matter of revelation, as much as any thing contained in the Bible. This is attested, as has been shown, by the whole nation of the Jews, to whom it was committed, and their fidelity to the truth has been avouched by the Lord and his Apostles. Is not this revelation? The integrity of the canon of the New Testament is equally a point of revelation. As God had said to the Jews, " Ye are my witnesses," and as they " received the lively oracles to give unto us," Acts, vii. 38; so the Lord Jesus said to the Apostles, " Ye shall be witnesses unto me, both in Jerusalem and all Judea, and in Samaria, and unto the uttermost part of the earth." The first churches received the New Testament Scriptures from these witnesses of the Lord, and thus had inspired authority for those books. It was not left to erudition or reasoning to collect, that they were a revelation from God. This the first Christians knew from the testimony of those who wrote them. They could not be more assured that the things taught were from God, than they were that the writings which contained them were from God. The integrity of the sacred canon is, then, a matter of revelation, conveyed to us by testimony, like every thing contained in the Scriptures.

While it has been denied that the question of the canon is a point of revelation, it has been asserted that it is a point of erudition. But erudition has nothing further to do with the question, than as it may be employed in conveying to us the testimony. Erudition did not produce the revelation of the canon.

If the canon had not been a point of revelation, erudition could never have made it so; for erudition can create nothing; it can only investigate and confirm truth, and testify to that which exists, or detect error. We receive the canon of Scripture by revelation, in the same way that the Jews received the law which was given from Mount Sinai. Only one generation of the Jews witnessed the giving of the law; but to all the future generations of that people, it was equally a matter of revelation. The knowledge of this was conveyed to them by testimony. In the same way, Christians, in their successive generations, receive the canon of Scripture as a matter of revelation. The testimony through which this is received, must indeed be translated from a foreign language; but so must the account brought to us of any occurrence the most trivial that takes place in a foreign country. If in this sense the question of the canon be called a point of erudition, the gospel itself must be called a point of erudition; for it, too, must be translated from the original language in which it was announced, as also must every thing which the Scriptures contain. When a preacher inculcates the belief of the gospel, or of a doctrine of Scripture, or obedience to any duty, would he be warranted in telling his audience that these are questions of erudition, not of Divine revelation? Erudition may be allowed its full value, without suspending on it the authority of the Word of God.

The assertion that the question of the canon is a point of erudition, not of Divine revelation, is subversive of the whole of revelation. We have no way of knowing that the miracles related in the Scriptures were wrought, and that the doctrines inculcated were taught, but by testimony and the internal evidence of the books themselves. We have the evidence of miracles, as that evidence comes to us by the testimony which vouches the authenticity of the inspired books. As far as the genuineness and authenticity of any book are brought into suspicion, so far is every thing contained in it brought into suspicion. For it should always be remembered, that there is no greater absurdity than to question the claim of a book to a place in the canon, and at the same time to acknowledge its contents to be a revelation from God. There can be no evidence that the doctrines of Scripture are revealed truths, unless we are certain that the books of Scripture are revelation. If the books which compose the canon are not matter of revelation, then we have no revelation. If the truth of the canon be not established to us as matter of revelation, then the books of which it is composed are not so established ; and if the books be not so, then not one sentence of them, nor one doctrine or precept which they contain, comes established to us as a revelation from God. If then the question of the canon be a point of erudition, not of Divine revelation, so is every doctrine which the Scriptures contain ; for the doctrine cannot be assured revelation, if the book that contains it be not assured revelation. There can be no higher evidence of the doctrine being revelation, than of the book that contains it ; and thus were not the canon a matter of Divine revelation, the whole Bible would be stripped of Divine authority. Any thing, therefore, that goes to unsettle the canon, goes to unsettle every doctrine contained in the canon.

Without a particular revelation to every individual, it does not appear that the authority of the canon could be ascertained to us in any other way than it is at present. The whole of the Scriptures was given at first by revelation, and afterwards this revelation was confirmed by ordinary means. The testimony concerning it has been handed down in the churches from one generation to another. On this, and on their own internal characteristics of being Divine, we receive the Scriptures with the most unsuspecting confidence, and on the same ground the Jews received the Scriptures of the Old Testament. In these ways, it is fixed by Divine authority, and not left in any uncertainty; for, if its truth can be ascertained by ordinary means, it is fixed by the authority of God, as much as if an angel from Heaven were every day to proclaim it over the earth. When Paul says, that his handwriting of the salutation was the token in every epistle, he at once shows us the importance of the canon, and warrants us in receiving it as a Divine revelation attested by ordinary means. Those to whom he wrote had no other way of knowing the handwriting of the Apostle than that by which they knew any other handwriting. Even at that time the churches knew the genuineness of the epistles sent to them by ordinary means; and Paul's authority warrants this as sufficient. We have, then, the authority of revelation for resting the canon on the ordinary sources of human evidence, and they are such as to preclude the possibility of deception. The claim of the Epistles sent to the first churches, and of the doctrine they contain as Divine, rested even to those churches on the same kind of evidence on which we now receive them. It is very important to settle what kind of evidence is sufficient for our receiving the Scriptures. Many have rated this too high; and as the Scriptures contain a revelation, they wished to have them attested to every age by revelation, which is, in fact, requiring the continuance of miraculous interference, which it might easily be shown would be pernicious.

With respect to the validity of the internal evidence on which the canon is received, an important argument may be founded on John, iv. 39. From the account of the woman of Samaria there related, we learn the kind of evidence on which the Lord Jesus was acknowledged while on earth. The foundation of this woman's faith was the Lord's having told her all things that ever she did. This was sufficient for her to recognise him as a prophet, or as one sent of God; and, consequently, when he declared to her that he was the Messiah, she had sufficient ground to believe so, for God would not enable any one to tell her such things in order to deceive. For if there was evidence from what he said that he was sent by God, there was evidence from his assertion that he was the Messiah. From verse 41 of the same chapter, we learn, that " many more believed because of his own word;" and that they did so, and that the woman believed, are exhibited to us, not only as facts, but as valid grounds of belief. Jesus had not worked any miracle, and the reason why they believed on him, is expressly stated to be because of his own word. If, then, the word of Jesus, unaccompanied by miracle, was a sufficient ground of faith when he spoke, it is equally valid in writing. From hearing him, the people of Samaria could assert, with confidence, that they themselves knew that he was indeed the Christ. And from reading the Scriptures, the same satisfactory evidence is obtained. In reading the Scriptures, we are often so struck with their evidence, that, independently of any other proof, we firmly believe that they come from God. We are often most forcibly convinced by evidence which we could hardly state intelligibly to others. The Apostles still commend themselves to every man's conscience, and we feel the force of the question, " What is the chaff to the wheat,—is not my word like a fire?" Must, then, the illiterate man receive the Scriptures as a question of erudition? Must the canonical authority of an epistle that recommends itself as the light of heaven, depend on questions of erudition?

Christians receive the Holy Scriptures on the authority of God, as declared by his inspired messengers, so that they are received on the ground of revelation. The illiterate are equally bound to receive them in this way, and interested in so doing, as the learned. As all are to be judged by them, it was necessary that all should have full assurance that they are from God; and it is matter of express revelation, that nothing but hatred of the light, and the love of darkness, prevents any man who reads them from receiving the truth. Both the Old Testament and the New come to us stamped with the authority of Him who is " the brightness of the Father's glory, and the express image of his person," and of those to whom God bore " witness both with signs and wonders, and diverse miracles, and gifts of the Holy Ghost," and also with their own internal evidence of being Divine. And if any portion of them be set aside as uninspired, or if any addition be made to them, it is done in spite of that authority and of that evidence.

If we displace from the canon any one of those books that have been sanctioned by the recognition of the Lord Jesus Christ and his Apostles, we overturn the authority on which the rest are held, and invite the evil propensities of our nature to quarrel with any thing in the Bible to which we find a disrelish. Those who hold that the question of the canon is open to discussion, and who set aside any part of it on the ground of either external or internal evidence, cannot be said to have a Bible. Their Bible will be longer or shorter, according to their researches; and a fixed standard they never can have.

If it be asked, should we be precluded from enquiring into the grounds on which the canon is received, it is replied, certainly not. But we should remember that the permanent ground on which it stands is testimony; and such must be the ground of every historical fact. Internal evidence may confirm the authenticity of a book sanctioned by the canon, but to suspend belief till we receive such confirmation, argues an ignorance of the principles of evidence. A book might be inspired, when no such internal confirmation, from the nature of the subject, might be found. And when a book is substantially approved, by testimony, as belonging to the canon, no evidence can, by a Christian, be legitimately supposed possible, in opposition to its inspiration. This would be to suppose valid objections to first principles. Sufficient testimony deserves the same rank as a first principle, with axioms themselves. Axioms are not more necessary than testimony, to all the business of human life. Internal evidence may be sufficient to prove that a book is not Divine; but it is absurd to suppose that such a book can have valid testimony, and therefore it can never be supposed by a Christian, that any of those books that are received as part of the sacred canon, on the authority of sufficient testimony, can contain any internal marks of imposture. This would be to suppose the possibility of the clashing of two first principles. The thing that can be proved by a legitimate first principle, can never be disproved by another legitimate first principle. This would be to suppose that God is not the author of the human constitution. If, then, in a book recognised by the canon, as the Song of Solomon, we find matter which to our wisdom does not appear to be worthy of inspiration, we may be assured that we mistake. For if that book is authenticated by testimony as a part of the sacred Scriptures, which the Lord Jesus Christ sanctioned, it is authenticated by a first principle, to which God has bound us, by the constitution of our nature, to submit. If, in this instance, or in any particular instance, we reject it, our own conduct in other things will be our condemnation. There is no first principle in the constitution of man that can lead him to reject any thing in the Song of Solomon, coming, as it does, under the sanction of a first principle. Those persons who reject any books of the canon on such grounds, would show themselves much more rational, as well as more humble Christians, if, recognising the paramount authority of a first principle universally acknowledged, they would receive the Song of Solomon and the Book of Esther, or any other of the books that they now reject, as parts of the Word of God, and humbly endeavour to gain from them the instruction and edification which, as Divine books, they must be calculated to give. This questioning of the canon, then, proceeds on infidel and irrational principles, which, if carried to their legitimate length, must end in complete unbelief.

"According to your way of proceeding," observes Augustine, in reference to those who supposed that the Scriptures had been interpolated or corrupted, and the observation is equally applicable to all who add to, or reject, certain parts of the sacred canon— "According to your way of proceeding, the authority of Scripture is quite destroyed, and every one's fancy is to determine what in the Scriptures is to be received, and what not. He does not admit it, because it is found in writings of so great credit and authority; but it is rightly written, because it is agreeable to his judgment. Into what confusion and uncertainty must men be brought by such a principle!"

It is a wonderful circumstance in the providence of God, that while the two parts of Scripture were delivered to two classes, with the fullest attestation of their Divine original, both the one and the other have been faithful in preserving the precious trust respectively committed to them, while they have both been rebellious in regard to that part of which they were not originally appointed the depositaries. The Jews always held the books of the Old Testament in the highest veneration, and continued to preserve them, without addition or diminution, until the coming of Him concerning whom they testify, and they have kept them entire to this day; yet they have altogether rejected the New Testament Scriptures. And while Christians have all agreed in preserving the Scriptures of the New Testament entire and uncorrupted, they have wickedly adulterated those of the Old by a spurious addition, or have retrenched certain portions of them. Of the Divine original of the Sacred Scriptures, as we now possess them, we have evidence the most abundant and diversified. It is the distinguishing characteristic of the Gospel, that it is preached to the poor, and God has so ordered it, that the authenticity of that Word by which all are to be judged, should not be presented to them as a matter of doubtful disputation.

Were there no other evidence of the truth of Divine revelation than the existence of the Holy Scriptures, that alone would be conclusive. The Bible is not a book compiled by a single author, nor by many authors, acting in confederacy in the same age, in which case it would not be so wonderful to find a just and close connexion in its several parts. It is the work of between thirty and forty writers in very different conditions of life, from the throne and sceptre down to the lowest degree, and in very distant ages, during which the world must have put on an entirely new appearance, and men must have had different interests to pursue. This would have led a spirit of imposture to vary its schemes, and to adapt them to different stations in the world, and to different fashions and changes in every age. David wrote about 400 years after Moses, and Isaiah about 250 after David, and John about 800 years after Isaiah. Yet these authors, with all the other Prophets and Apostles, wrote in perfect harmony, confirming the authority of their predecessors, labouring to enforce their instructions, and denouncing the severest judgments on all who continued disobedient. Such entire agreement in propounding religious truths and principles, different from any before or since promulgated, except by those who have learned from them, establishes the Divine mission of the writers of the Bible beyond dispute, proving that they all derived their wisdom from God, and spake as they were moved by the Holy Ghost. In all the works of God there is an analogy characteristic of his Divine hand; and the variety and harmony that shine so conspicuously in the heavens and the earth, are not farther removed from the suspicion of imposture than the unity that, in the midst of boundless variety, reigns in that book which reveals the plan of redemption. To forge the Bible is as impossible as to forge a world.

THE INSPIRATION OF THE HOLY SCRIPTURES.

The Scriptures of the Old and New Testaments are not only genuine and authentic, but also inspired writings. The claim of inspiration which they advance, is a claim of infallibility and of perfection. It is also a claim of absolute authority, which demands unlimited submission. It is a claim which, if set up for any other book, might, with the utmost ease, be shown to be unfounded.

The inspiration of the Scriptures is attested, both by the nature and value of their contents, and by the evidence of their truth. On these grounds, they stand without a rival in the world, and challenge from every man the highest possible regard.

Our knowledge of the inspiration of the Bible, like every other doctrine it contains, must be collected from itself. If the writers of this book appear with such credentials as entitle them to be received as commissioned of God, then it is from themselves only that we can learn those truths which they are authorized to make known. Among these, it is of primary importance to know what is the extent of that dependence which we are to place on their words.

Is implicit credit to be given to every thing they declare? and, if the writers are numerous, is this equally due to them all?

The question of inspiration has been viewed as one of the utmost difficulty; and, accordingly, various theories have been invented to explain it. To those who consider the subject merely in the light of the Bible itself, (the only source of legitimate information on any matter of revelation,) it may appear surprising that this doctrine should be supposed to present any difficulties at all. Nothing can be more clearly, more expressly, or more precisely taught in the Word of God. And while other important doctrines may be met with passages of seeming opposition, there is not in the language of the Scriptures one expression that even appears to contradict their plenary or verbal inspiration. Whence, then, it may be asked, has arisen the idea of difficulty so general among the learned, but utterly unknown to the great body of Christians. It has wholly arisen from a profane desire to penetrate into the manner of the Divine operation on the mind of man in the communication of revealed truth. Instead of coming to the Scriptures in a childlike manner, and humbly submitting to what they teach on this subject, many have occupied themselves in forming a scale for determining how far Divine assistance was afforded to the sacred penman in the different parts of their writings; and, according to almost all those who have discussed this subject, some parts of Scripture require only a very small degree of Divine assistance. But as the Scriptures assert the inspiration equally of all their parts, these writers are obliged to denominate even this slight assistance as a kind of inspiration. Some, accordingly, make three degrees or kinds of inspiration, while others add a fourth. To the *Superintendence, Elevation,* and *Suggestion,* of Doddridge, has been added *Direction.** And some, substantially agreeing in the doctrine of different degrees, quarrel with the terms by which these distinctions are designated, and for Suggestion have substituted *Revelation,* as more appropriately expressing the highest degree in the scale of inspiration.

To these speculations, though very generally adopted, the writers of the Scriptures give not the slightest countenance or support. Such being the fact, and as the question of inspiration can only be determined by the Scriptures themselves, all the distinctions that have been introduced are nothing better than vain and unsubstantial theories, unfounded and unsupported by any evidence. The Scriptures contain no intimation of their being written under an inspiration of any kind but one. "*All Scripture,*" says Paul, "*is given by inspiration of God.*" This declaration refers to the whole of the Old Testament, which Timothy had known from his

---

* For these distinctions there is no foundation whatever. Superintendence, Elevation, and Direction, are not degrees of the inspiration of Scripture. Had these been all enjoyed by the writers of the Bible, it would not have made it an inspired book, nor have entitled it to be called the Word of God.

childhood. But as the greater part of the New Testament was at that time published, and as the whole of it is uniformly classed by its writers with the Old Testament, this expression of Paul equally applies to the New Testament. The Apostle Peter classes *all* the Epistles of Paul, which he ascribes to the wisdom given to him, with " the other Scriptures," thereby declaring them to be of the same authority, and showing that all the writings, both of the Old and New Testament, were designated the " Scriptures."

Inspiration belongs to the original writings. No one contends for any degree of inspiration in the transcribers in different ages. Accuracy in the copies they have made is, under the providence of God, by which he always perfectly attains his purposes, secured by the fidelity of those to whom the Scriptures have been committed—by the opposition of parties watching each other, as of Jews and Christians, and of various sects—and by the great multiplication of copies and translations into different languages, which took place so early.

The inspiration spoken of in the book of Job, xxxii. 8, where it is said, " There is a spirit in men, and the inspiration of the Almighty giveth them understanding," appears to refer to the communication of those intellectual powers with which man is endowed by his Creator. Every Christian has, besides this, an unction from the Holy Ghost, who dwelleth in him, through whom he was born again, and by whose influence his spiritual life is maintained. There have also been various miraculous gifts of the Holy Spirit bestowed on the servants of God, and among these is that inspiration, by means of which God has revealed himself in the Scriptures of the Old and New Testaments.

The word *inspire* signifies to breathe into, and literally corresponds to the original in 2 Tim. iii. 16. All *Scripture is inspired by God*, or *breathed into the writers by God*. It is, therefore, of the *writing* that the inspiration is asserted. The Greek compound word, corresponding to our phrase *inspired by God*, was applied among the heathens to such dreams as were supposed to be breathed into men by any of the gods. This inspiration, which, without any exception, variation, or gradation, is claimed by the writers of the Scripture, and which entitles the whole of it to be denominated "the Word of God," is of the highest kind by which they were "led into all truth." It consists in that communication made to their minds by the Spirit of God, of the ideas and words which they have recorded in that sacred book. Paul expressly calls the Old Testament Scriptures " the ORACLES of God," which were committed to the Jews.—Rom. iii. 2. He afterwards gives the same denomination of " oracles" to all the revealed truth of God.— Heb. v. 12. The same expression was used by the Greeks to denote the responses given out in distinct words, which their priests made, in name of their deities, to those who consulted them. In the same sense, Stephen, speaking under the immediate influence of the Holy Ghost, designates the writings of

Moses as "lively oracles." In this expression their *verbal* inspiration is distinctly asserted.

In the passage above quoted, "*All Scripture is given by inspiration of God,*" the same thing is distinctly affirmed. Paul does not say the *meaning* of all Scripture, or the *ideas* contained in it, but all *Scripture*—all *writing*, or all that is *written* (taking writing in the appropriated sense in which he uses it) is given by inspiration of God. We have here a most unequivocal testimony to the inspiration of the *words* of Scripture, for neither a meaning, nor an idea, can be expressed in writing, except by words. If any writing is inspired, the words of necessity must be inspired, because the words are the writing; for what is a writing, but words written? The thoughts and sentiments are the meaning of the words. To say that a writing is inspired, while the *words* are uninspired, is a contradiction in terms. The affirmation of Paul, then, respects the words as containing the meaning, and not the meaning as containing the words. To the same purpose, the Apostle Peter affirms, that "*the prophecy came not of old time* [at any time] *by the will of man, but holy men of God spake as they were moved by the Holy Ghost.*" If they *spake* as they were *moved*, they did not choose the language they uttered, but the words which they spoke were given to them by the Holy Ghost. In the same manner the disciples, on the day of Pentecost, "*were all filled with the Holy Ghost, and began to speak with other tongues, as the Spirit gave them utterance.*" Here *utterance*, or the words they spoke, is expressly ascribed to the Holy Spirit. Nothing can more distinctly convey the meaning of inspiration than these words, " *who by the mouth of thy servant David hast said.*" — Acts, iv. 25. And this inspiration, which without variation or exception is claimed for the Scriptures, by the sacred writers, entitles the whole of them to be called " *the Word of God*," to which high designation they could not be entitled on any other ground.

The words of Scripture, as used by the writers, were indeed their own words. But this does not imply that the Bible is partly the word of God, and partly the word of man. It is not the effect of any such co-operation, as supposes that one part was produced by God, and the other part by man, to make out a whole. The passages above quoted preclude our entertaining any such notion. Because the words were written by the Prophets and Apostles, this does not prevent them from being the words of God. The following remarks of President Edwards, when he is combating the deeply erroneous sentiment of the Arminians, respecting a co-operation between God and man in the work of grace, will explain this matter. " In efficacious grace we are not merely passive, nor yet does God do some, and we do the rest. But God does all, and we do all. God produces all, and we act all. For that is what he produces, viz. our own acts. God is the only proper author and foundation: we only are the proper actors. We are, in different respects, wholly passive and wholly active. In the Scriptures the same things are represented as from God and from us. God is said to convert, and men are said to convert and turn. God makes a new heart, and we are commanded to make us a new heart. God circumcises the heart, and we are commanded to circumcise our own hearts; not merely because we must use the means in order to the effect, but the effect itself is our act and our duty. These things are agreeable to that text, ' God worketh in you both to will and to do.' "—Edwards's Remarks, &c. 251.

" We grant," says Dr Owen, " that they" (the sacred writers) " used their own *abilities of mind* and understanding in the choice of words and expressions. So the *preacher* sought to find out *acceptable words*, Eccles. xii. 10. But the Holy Spirit, who is more intimate into the minds and skill of men than they are themselves, did so guide and operate in them, as that the words they fixed upon were as directly and certainly from him, as if they had been spoken to them by an audible voice."—Owen on the Spirit, Book ii. chap. i. sect. 20.

We are not, however, required to suppose, that while inspired, the ordinary exercise of the faculties of the penmen of the Scriptures was counteracted or suspended, or that their minds did not entirely go along with what was communicated to them. " They were all filled with the Holy Ghost," Acts xi. 4. They " had the mind of Christ," 1 Cor. xi. 15; and were themselves cast into the mould of that doctrine which they delivered to others. We are certain, then, as appears from the whole of their writings, that as far as they comprehended the truths which they were employed to record, they both fully acquiesced in them, and powerfully felt their force. It forms no objection to their inspiration, that the words of Scripture are occasionally changed in parallel passages or quotations, by Him who dictated them. The Holy Spirit is not confined to any one mode of expression, and in such places his mind is conveyed in words, which, though varied by him, are yet perfectly adapted to communicate his will.

Nor does the difference of style which we find among these writers at all conclude against their having the words they were to write imparted to them. On the same ground that the term " Scripture" includes the thoughts and words, so also does it necessarily comprehend the style in which it is written; which is in fact nothing more than the choice and arrangement of the words; for what is style, abstracted from the words that express it? The style that God was pleased to employ was used, and the instruments were such as that style was natural to, flowing, like the words, with their full consent, and according to the particular tone of their minds. The style of the Scriptures is the characteristic style of the different writers; but God is the author of it. The style is as truly God's as the matter; for if he has employed the style of different writers, he has likewise employed their expressions, thoughts, reasonings, and arguments. God did not leave them to the operation of their own mind, but has employed the operations of their mind in his word. The Holy Spirit could dictate to them his own words in such a way that they would also be their own words, uttered with the understanding. He could express the same thought by the mouth of a thousand persons, each in his own style. Is it then because we cannot comprehend the mode of such an operation, that arrogant and weak mortals dare to deny the obvious import of Scripture declarations?

The objection to verbal inspiration, taken from the variety of style among the sacred writers, or from the circumstance that the same fact is often variously related by them, though at first sight it may seem plausible, is, in reality, both unfounded and absurd. It is taking it for granted that two or more accounts of the same thing, differing in phraseology, though substantially agreeing, cannot all be the words of inspiration; which has not the smallest foundation in truth. If variety of expression in relating the same things in the Gospel, would not affect the truth of the narrative, on the supposition that the writers were uninspired men, why is it presumed that it would affect it on the supposition of their being inspired? and why should it be thought improper for the Holy Ghost to make use of that variety? Or, because one peculiar cast of style distinguished every man's writings, is it thought impossible that the Spirit of God can employ a variety of styles; or is it supposed that He must be confined to one single mode of expression? The simple statement of such an idea contains its refutation. It is evident, too, that variety of style militates no more against verbal inspiration, than against the supposed inspiration of *superintendence;* for if the Holy Spirit *sanctioned* variety, it was equally consistent to *dictate* variety. And it might be shown that such variety is of essential importance in the Gospel narratives in bringing out very interesting views, that could not be so well exhibited in a single narrative.

Of the fact, however, that the variety of style which is found among the writers of the Scriptures does not in the smallest degree militate against that verbal inspiration by which they affirm that they wrote, we have conclusive proof. For while it is evident to all, that there is a certain characteristic distinction of style, that pervades the whole of the Scriptures, and sufficiently attests that they are the work of the same author, it is equally certain that each one of the writers is distinguished from the rest by a style peculiar to himself. Now the difference of style is as great among the prophets, when predicting future events which they did not understand, where, *as is admitted by all, the words they employed must necessarily have been communicated to them*, as it is found to be among them when relating events with which they were previously acquainted. Here, then, we have positive proof on this subject, which it is impossible to set aside. The objection, too, that is founded on variety of style, to the communication of *words*, would equally militate against the communication of *ideas*. *There is as great diversity of* MODES OF THOUGHT, *and of viewing their subjects, as of* EXPRESSION AND STYLE, *among the writers of Scripture*. And can it for a moment be supposed, that either as to the one or the other, the Spirit of God is limited? " He that planted the ear, shall he not hear? He that formed the eye, shall he not see?" " Who hath made man's mouth, or who maketh the dumb, or the deaf, or the seeing, or the blind, did not I the Lord?" He who conferred upon men all the varied powers and faculties which they possess, is he not able to communicate to their minds whatever to him seems good, in every possible variety of expression, and in every conceivable shape?

It has been objected, that if the verbal inspiration of the whole of the Scriptures could be proved, it would follow, that the words of all the speakers who are introduced in them, such as those of Job's friends, although their opinions were erroneous, nay even the words of the devil himself, were inspired. This objection is so absurd, that, unless it had been sometimes gravely urged, it would be too trifling to be noticed. Is it not sufficiently plain, that while God dictated to the sacred penman the words of those referred to, he dictated them to be inserted, not as *his* words, but as *their* words? Even the sayings of wicked men and of devils in the Scriptures are recorded by inspiration as truly as the sayings of Christ himself, and, as recorded by the Holy Ghost, suggest inspired instruction. Every thing contained in the Bible, whether the words of the penman, that contain the mind of God, or the words of others, that are inserted for the purpose of giving such information as he is pleased to impart, is equally, according to the express declarations of Scripture, dictated by God. It should, however, be observed, that it is not at all implied in the assertion of plenary verbal inspiration, that every example recorded in Scripture, without any judgment expressed with regard to the conduct of good, or even inspired men, should be for imitation. When the Word of God records human conduct, without pronouncing on its morality, whether it is sin or duty must be ascertained by an appeal to the general principles of Scripture.

It is no valid objection to verbal inspiration, that the sacred writers were often acquainted beforehand with those facts which they recorded, and that they were directed to refer to this knowledge to establish their credibility. This no more proves that their relating these facts originated with themselves, than the previous knowledge of a messenger of the contents of the message he bears, proves that it originated with himself, or detracts from its truth or authority. Nor does it form any objection that the penmen of Scripture often appeal, in support of what they advance, to its own evidence, or that they reason from principles granted by those whom they addressed. This was practised by the Lord himself, as to whose words no Christian will affirm that they are not the words of God.

There is a simplicity, harmony, and consistency, in that plan which represents the Scriptures as, in one point of view, the production of man, and in another wholly the book of God. This is precisely consistent with the language of the Apostle Paul, when he sometimes designates the Gospel, " my Gospel," and sometimes, " the Gospel of God," it being, in fact, both the one and the other. Though the deepest wisdom of man could never have anticipated such a scheme of inspiration, yet when it is submitted to the mind, it manifests itself to be Divine. And nothing but this view will harmonize all the assertions of the Scriptures.

The subject of the inspiration of the Bible has been too much disregarded among Christians; many have not attended to it at all, while others have ventured to indulge in vain speculations respecting it. But like every other doctrine, the nature of Divine inspiration ought to be carefully enquired into, and the truth respecting it received with the most unreserved submission. It will be proper, then, to consider it solely in the light which the Word of God affords; and for this purpose, after attending to the objections that have been derived from erroneous views of the meaning of certain passages of Scripture, to exhibit the ample proofs contained in the sacred record, which unequivocally substantiate its own plenary inspiration in every part, without a single exception.

The inspiration of certain parts of the Scriptures is frequently denied, on the supposition that the Apostles themselves " sometimes candidly admit, that they are not speaking by inspiration." This objection proceeds on a mistaken view of the meaning of the passages on which it is founded.

In the 7th chapter of the 1st Epistle to the Corinthians, the Apostle Paul is supposed, in some places, to disclaim inspiration, and, in one place, not to be certain whether or not he is inspired. This, at first sight, will appear to be evidently contrary to the uniform style of this Apostle's writings, and altogether improbable, when, as a commissioned and accredited ambassador of Jesus Christ, he is answering certain questions put to him by a Christian church, to whom he had just before in the most explicit manner asserted, that he spoke "not in the words which man's wisdom teacheth, but which the Holy Ghost teacheth;" and that he was addressing them "in the name of the Lord Jesus." 1 Cor. ii. 13, and v. 4. Attention to this might have prevented the adoption of the unfounded and mistaken meaning that has been affixed to the passages referred to, which tends to unsettle the minds of Christians respecting the inspiration of the Scriptures. No such indecision, however, attaches to the passages in question.

In answer to the question about marriage, Paul says, 1 Cor. vii. 6, "*I speak this by permission, and not of commandment.*" Does this mean that the Spirit permitted him, but did not command him, to give the answer he had done? Even upon this supposition, the Apostle's declaration must be according to the mind of the Spirit: for Paul could not, on such an occasion, have been permitted to say what was contrary to it. But this would have been a very extraordinary and unusual mode of communicating that mind, and evidently is not what is here intended. The obvious meaning is, that what the Apostle here said was in the way of permission, not of commandment. "I speak this," says he, "as a permission, and not as a commandment;" and without this, the Apostle might have been understood as enjoining marriage as an indispensable duty. In the second Epistle to the same church, chap. viii. 8, the Apostle expresses himself to the same purpose, in a passage which no one misunderstands. Again, at the 10th verse,—" *Unto the married I command, yet not I, but the Lord.*" This commandment had been delivered by the Lord Jesus Christ himself. The Apostle, therefore, had no new commandment to deliver to them, or no commandment from himself only, but one which the Lord had given. " *To the rest, speak I, not the Lord.*" There was no former commandment given by the Lord, to which he might here refer them; on this point, therefore, he now delivers to them the will of God. So far, indeed, was this commandment from having been given before, that it was the repeal of an old one, by which, under the Jewish dispensation, the people were commanded to put away their wives, if heathens. Can it, then, be supposed, that the Apostle is speaking from himself, and not under the dictation of the Holy Ghost, when he is declaring the abrogation of a part of the law of God?

" *Now, concerning virgins, I have no commandment of the Lord; yet I give my judgment as one that hath obtained mercy of the Lord to be faithful.*" Here again no commandment had formerly been given, to which Paul could refer those to whom he wrote. But now, he gave his judgment as one that had obtained mercy of the Lord to be faithful in the discharge of that ministry which he had received, to deliver the whole counsel of God to man. " *I think also that I have the Spirit of God.*" In this, as in many other passages, the word translated, "I think,"*

---

* " On 1 Cor. vii. 40, *Wolfius* remarks, that the v. οκω imports not an uncertain opinion, but conviction and knowledge,

does not mean doubting, but the most positive certainty. If Paul meant it to be understood, that he was not certain whether he was inspired or not, it would contradict all that he has positively affirmed in the same Epistle, on the subject of his inspiration, both before the expression in question, and afterwards, when he says, chap. xiv. 37, " If any man think himself to be a prophet, or spiritual, let him acknowledge that *the things which I write unto you are the commandments of the Lord.*" And it would stand directly opposed to what he affirms, 1 Thess. iv. 8, " He, therefore, that despiseth, despiseth not man, but God, who hath also given unto us his Holy Spirit." But so far is this from being the case, that in order more deeply to impress the minds of those to whom he wrote, with the importance of what he had said, Paul concludes by assuring them that he was *certain* that he wrote by the Spirit of God.

The only other passage in which this Apostle is supposed to disclaim inspiration, occurs in 2 Cor. xi. 17 :—" *That which I speak, I speak it not after the Lord, but as it were foolishly, in this confidence of boasting.*" In this passage Paul does not refer to the authority, but to the example of the Lord. " I speak not according to the example or manner of the Lord,

---

as John v. 39. So in *Xenophon*, Cyroped., at the end of the proem, Ησθνσθαι ΔΟΚΟΥΜΕΝ, expresses *assurance*, not doubt."—PARKHURST. And see Acts xxvi. 9 ; 1 Cor. iv. 9 ; " Doth he thank that servant because he did the things that were commanded him ? *I trow not.*" Luke xvii. 9.

but after the manner of fools:" a manner which, as he tells the Corinthians in the next chapter, they had compelled him to adopt. Such is the true sense of the above passages ; but even if the mistaken meaning so often attributed to them were the just one, they would not at all militate against the plenary inspiration of the Scriptures, because in that case Paul was inspired to write precisely as he has done, since they form a part of Scripture, *all* of which *is given by inspiration of God."* If he has told us that he was not inspired on these points, he was inspired to make the denial.

Another passage in the Second Epistle of Peter, i. 19, is frequently quoted, so as to invalidate the Apostolic testimony. Peter had just before affirmed, that on the mount of transfiguration, he and the other Apostles had been eyewitnesses of the majesty of Jesus Christ, and had heard the voice from heaven, which attested that he was the beloved Son of God. Yet, after this, he is supposed to refer Christians to the word of prophecy, as " more sure" than this testimony. Instead of this, which affixes a meaning to the passage degrading to the testimony of the Apostles, (than which there is nothing in heaven, or on earth, more absolutely certain,) he refers to the prophecies, now made " confirmed" by what they had witnessed.*

---

* " He," the Apostle, " does not oppose," says *Wetstein*, " the prophetic word to fables, or to the transfiguration seen by himself. . . . But the prophetic word is *more firm* now, as it has been confirmed by the event, than it was before the event. So the Greek interpreters understood the passage."—Parkhurst.

Two passages are quoted from Paul's First Epistle to Timothy, v. 23, " *Drink no longer water, but use a little wine for thy stomach's sake, and thine often infirmities.*" And 2 Tim. iv. 13, " *The cloak that I left at Troas with Carpus, when thou comest, bring with thee, and the books, but especially the parchments.*" These passages, it is supposed, are of so unimportant a nature, that they cannot be the dictates of inspiration. Such a conclusion, even if we could not discover their use, would be altogether unwarrantable. On the same principle we might reject many other parts of Scripture, the import of which we do not understand; but, in doing so, we should act both as absurdly and irreverently as the daring infidel, who might assert that a worm or a mushroom was not the workmanship of God, because it appeared to him insignificant; or that the whole world was not created by God, because it contained deserts and barren wastes, the use of which he could not comprehend.

" The different truths of revelation," says Mr Carew, " have a different degree of importance; but it requires as much inspiration to tell what hour it is by inspiration, as to reveal the Gospel itself. If all Scripture is given by inspiration, the reference to Paul's cloak requires as much inspiration, as those passages that declare the way of salvation. The question is not, whether many things in Scripture might have been known without inspiration, as there are unquestionably others that could not at all have been otherwise known: But the question is, whether the most trivial thing said to be inspired, can be inspired in any other sense than things of the utmost moment. As long as it stands recorded, " All Scripture is given by inspiration of God," so long the honour of revelation is as much concerned in the inspiration of an incidental allusion, as in that of the most fundamental truth."*

---

* " The question is, not at all whether the Apostle Paul needed inspiration to enable him to give such directions, but whether it was without inspiration that these doctrines form a part of a book, *all* of which comes to us as the Word of God, and inspired by him. There are many parts of Scripture that might have been written without inspiration ; but the question is, were the sacred writers left without inspiration to select what they would put into this book, and what they would keep out of it ? If so, then the book is their's, not God's. Besides, if it be thought absurd to suppose that there is any inspiration in the direction which the Apostle gives about his cloak and his books, it may very naturally be thought that as little inspiration was necessary to tell us how often he had received forty stripes save one ; that he had fought with wild beasts at Ephesus ; that he had undergone an endless variety of perils; that he had been let down over the wall of Damascus in a basket, and put in the stocks at Philippi. Of all these, and many other similar instances, it may be said, that these are cases in which, as it would be absurd to suppose any inspiration, so it was unnecessary to disavow it. We shall thus get quit of the whole account of the sufferings of the Apostles. The Apostle says, that ' All Scripture is given by inspiration of God, and is profitable,' &c. If there be many passages, or any passage, in which it would be absurd to suppose any inspiration, or which is not profitable, then he is guilty of stating what is not true."

In reference to the above passages, Dr Doddridge makes the following remarks : " There are *other objections* of a quite different class, with which I have no concern ; because they affect only *such a degree of inspiration* as I think it *not prudent*, and I am sure it is *not necessary*, to assert. I leave them, therefore, to be *answered by those*, if any such there be, who imagine that *Paul* would need *an immediate Revelation* from Heaven, and a miraculous dictate of the *Holy Ghost*, to remind *Timothy of the cloak and writings which he left at Troas*, or to advise him to *mingle a little wine with his water*."* Modern writers on inspiration have likewise singled out these two passages, together with the shipwreck of Paul on the island of Melita, as uninspired, because they conceive that " these were not things of a religious nature."

Respecting the account of the Apostle's shipwreck, there are few things to be found in the historical part of the Bible that are more truly valuable, whether we consider the encouraging view it affords of the providential dealings of the Lord in every circumstance of the life of his people, or attend to the unparalleled illustration it furnishes of the manner by which the purposes of God are, in the use of means, carried into effect. Nothing could be more worthy of inspiration than the recording of this portion of Scripture ; and so far from not being of a religious

---

* Dissertation on the Inspiration of the New Testament, in Appendix to the Harmony of the Evangelists, p. 58.

nature, the account it contains is fraught with the most important religious instruction. The objection founded on the two passages in the Epistles to Timothy, being commonly resorted to as one of the *strongholds* of those who oppose the verbal inspiration of the whole of Scripture, requires to be examined at some length. Instead of being so trifling as to render them unworthy to be a part of Divine Revelation, they present considerations of very high interest.

In the first of these passages, it is said, "*Drink no longer water, but use a little wine for thy stomach's sake, and thine often infirmities.*" A due consideration of the nature of the office of Paul, who gave this injunction to Timothy, and of the Epistle in which it is contained, as a part of the oracles of God, as well as of the service in which Timothy was engaged, ought to have deterred any one from rashly concluding that this verse forms no part of the words of inspiration. The connexion, too, in which it is found, embodied in one of the most solemn addresses to be met with in the Scriptures, assures us that it must contain something of importance. "*I charge thee before God, and the Lord Jesus Christ, and the elect angels, that thou observe these things, without preferring one before another, doing nothing by partiality. Lay hands suddenly on no man, neither be partaker of other men's sins: keep thyself pure. Drink no longer water, but use a little wine for thy stomach's sake, and thine often infirmities. Some men's sins are open beforehand,*

THE HOLY SCRIPTURES. 131

going before to judgment; and some men they follow after. Likewise also the good works of some are manifest beforehand; and they that are otherwise cannot be hid." Can it be imagined that,—in the midst of an address, in which, if the language of inspiration is to be found in the Bible, the Apostle is speaking by it,—before the charge is completed, which contains a permanent law in the kingdom of Christ, the course of that inspiration is suddenly interrupted, and broken in upon, by a remark merely human, " not of a religious nature,"—by an advice, which, originating with the Apostle, might not be judicious? On the contrary, being fully assured that the verse in question is, like the other parts of the charge that precede and follow it, dictated by the Divine Spirit, we are prepared to regard it as containing what is worthy of its author, and deserving of our attention. Proceeding, then, to examine it, under the settled conviction that it is given by inspiration of God, and that it is profitable for instruction in righteousness, I observe, 1. That while enjoining upon Timothy many arduous and laborious duties, the Apostle was inspired to admonish him to attend to his health, in order to fit him for their right discharge; and hence Timothy was taught, and we learn, that it is the duty of every man to have a regard for his health, even amidst the most important labours, in order that he may be more fitted for the service of God, and that his life may be prolonged in that service.

2. We learn the abstemiousness of Timothy, not-

withstanding his bodily weakness, and abundant labours.

3. That his abstemiousness was even carried the length of an unnecessary austerity, and that although he had a good end in view, this over-abstemiousness was wrong, and was therefore corrected by the Apostle. Hence, we learn how apt we are to err, even when our intentions are good, and how necessary it is to receive direction from the Lord.

4. If Timothy was in an error respecting the lawfulness of using wine, that error is here corrected; but whether this was the case or not, it was a matter of importance to instruct believers on this point, on which, as it appears from Rom. xiv. 21, a diversity of opinion existed in the churches. The lawfulness of the use of wine was denied by the Essenes, a sect among the Jews, as was afterwards the case with different Christian sects. This error may have been imbibed by them, or confirmed by the law of the Nazarites, or from a partial attention to the manner in which the Rechabites, who abstained from wine, were held up as an example of obedience to the people of Israel. In this view of the passage, it contains a most salutary and necessary corrective of what might otherwise have become extensively prejudicial in the kingdom of Christ; and it proves a useful comment, in the way of warning, on what the Apostle had said a little before, concerning a defection that was to take place in the latter times, in which false teachers were to command men to abstain from meats which God had created, to be received with thanksgiving, chap. iii. 3.

5. Use " a little wine." Here we are instructed in the duty of temperance. We are taught to use the bounties of Providence with moderation, and in subordination to our sustenance and bodily health.

6. If the error of those who live too abstemiously, so as to injure their health, be here corrected; how much more does this passage condemn those who exceed in a contrary extreme, and who impair their constitution by intemperance!

7. From this passage, as from some others, *e. g.* Phil. ii. 27, we learn that the Apostles had it not in their power on every occasion, even when they might be desirous of it, to work miraculous cures, and that the gift of healing, at that time vouchsafed, did not preclude the use of means for the preservation of health.

8. This passage sanctions the medical profession. This is very important, as some Christians have been inclined to think, that to have recourse to a physician is to supersede the interposition of God. Now, the prescription of Paul to Timothy was a medical prescription, founded on the fitness of the medicinal qualities of wine. Christians ought, indeed, to look to God for their cure, so ought they for the nourishment of their bodies, for man does not live by bread alone; but both food and *medicine* are to be taken as the means appointed by God, as we here learn.

The other passage referred to, occurs in Paul's Second Epistle to Timothy, ch. iv. 13. "*The cloak that I left at Troas with Carpus, when thou comest, bring with thee, and the books, but especially the parchments.*" This passage, like the former, is introduced in the midst of very solemn considerations, in connexion with an annunciation of the Apostle Paul's trial for his life, and in the immediate prospect of his martyrdom. In his desire to have his cloak brought to him from a distance, a proof is recorded at the close of his ministry, of Paul's disinterestedness in his labours among the churches. We are here reminded of his resolution, and are taught how faithfully he adhered to it, to make the Gospel of God without charge; and in the peculiar circumstances in which he was placed, not to abuse his power of receiving support in preaching the Gospel, or to allow his glorying on the ground of his disinterestedness to be made void, 1 Cor. ix. 13-18. On the approach of winter, in a cold prison, and at the termination of his course, the Apostle Paul appears here to be a follower indeed of him who had not where to lay his head. He is presented to our view as actually enduring those hardships, which elsewhere he describes in a manner so affecting—" in prisons,—in cold,—in nakedness." He had abandoned, as he elsewhere informs us, all the fair prospects that once opened to him of worldly advantages, for the excellency of the knowledge of Christ, and had suffered the loss of all things: and in this Epistle we see all that he has said on the subject, embodied and verified. He is about to suffer death for the testimony of Jesus; and now he requests one of the few friends that still adhered to him (all the others, as he tells us, having forsaken him) to do his diligence to come before winter, and to bring to him his cloak. Here, in his solemn farewell address, of which the verse before us forms a part,—the last of his writings, and which contains a passage of unrivalled grandeur,—the Apostle of the Gentiles is exhibited in a situation deeply calculated to affect us. We behold him standing upon the confines of the two worlds,—in this world about to be beheaded, as guilty, by the Emperor of Rome,—in the other world to be crowned, as righteous, by the King of kings,—here deserted by men, there to be welcomed by angels,—here in want of a cloak to cover him, there to be clothed upon with his house from heaven.

Dr Doddridge, in his commentary on the passage before us, has the following note. "*Bring with thee that cloak.* If φελονην here signifies *cloak*, or *mantle*, it is, as *Grotius* justly observes, a proof of *Paul's* poverty, that he had occasion to send so far for such a garment, which probably was not quite a new one." Since, as we here learn, this observation of Grotius appeared *just* to Dr Doddridge, it might have prevented him from rashly treating the subject with the levity which appears in his remark, formerly quoted, and from *thinking* it not "prudent" to assert, that the text was dictated by the Holy Spirit. The observation of Grotius, to which he refers, is as follows: " See the poverty of so great an Apostle, who considered so small a matter, left at such a distance, to be a loss to him!" On the same place, Erasmus remarks: " Behold the Apostle's household furniture, a cloak to defend him from rain, and a few books !" Here, then, we are reminded incidentally (a manner of instruction common in the Word of God) of Paul's poverty. In the low, distressed circumstances of the

Apostles, we see the Lord's warnings, as to the reception they were to meet with from the world, and the hardships and privations they were to experience, fully verified. The evidence of the truth of the Gospel, which arises from the suffering condition of those who were first employed to propagate it, is calculated to produce on our minds the strongest conviction of its Divine origin. In the wisdom of God it appears to have been appointed for this end; and it is all along kept in view, in the accounts transmitted in the Scriptures concerning them. "I think that God hath set forth us the Apostles last, as it were appointed unto death ; for we are made a spectacle unto the world, and to angels, and to men. Even unto this present hour we both hunger, and thirst, and are naked, and are buffeted, and have no certain dwelling-place." 1 Cor. iv. 9-11.

Paul also desires Timothy to bring with him the " books, but especially the parchments." Whatever these parchments were, the use that Paul intended to make of them would be well known to Timothy, and in it he might have a further example of the Apostle's zeal, and unwearied exertion in the service of God. By this passage we may be taught, that even those who were so highly favoured with the most distinguished gifts, were not raised above the necessity of using means for their own improvement, and for the stirring up of those gifts that were in them ; and if this was the case respecting them, how forcibly is the duty here inculcated upon us, to give diligence to retain the knowledge of Divine things which we may already possess, and to seek to add to our present attainments, whatever we may suppose them to be! We are certain that they were not useless books, which the Apostle required to be brought to him at such a time, and from so great a distance. They must have been intended to be profitable to himself, or in some way to be turned to the advancement of that cause, to promote which was his only desire, and for which he was now about to suffer. In any, or all of these views, the contents of this verse may convey instruction, and afford an example to us; and at any rate we can no more conceive that the course of inspiration is here interrupted, without the smallest intimation to this effect, (of which an example in the whole Bible cannot be produced,) than we can believe it was the case concerning the verse which we formerly considered.

In the former of the above passages, we observe Paul evincing his kindness and sympathy, and attending to the wants of a fellow labourer; in the latter, to his own wants. Is there any thing in either of them beneath the dignity of Divine Revelation? In prescribing, by his Apostle, the use of wine, which he would bless for the re-establishment of the health of Timothy, the Lord acted in the same manner as when he directed his Prophet to order the application of "a lump of figs," for the cure of King Hezekiah. Was it beneath the dignity of Him who turned water into wine at a marriage feast, to order the use of wine for the preservation of Timothy's health, instead of the use of water? Was this unworthy of that Lord who had condescended so far to the indulgence of the feelings of his people, as to cause it to be engrossed in his law, that the man who had planted a vineyard, and had not eaten of it, should not go out to war, lest he should die in the battle? Deut. xx. 6.

So far from there being any thing in these passages beneath the dignity of a revelation from God, or unworthy of his character, they are entirely consistent with the one, and strikingly illustrative of the other. And it is only when we consider them, not as the word of man, but as " *the Word of God,*" that we discover their beauty and their use. It is God himself who there speaks. He who is the high and lofty One that inhabiteth eternity, condescends to the weakness and to the wants of his servants. Nothing that interests them escapes his notice. The hairs of their head are all numbered, and the smallest circumstance of their lot is ordered by the providence of God. What a striking illustration do these two passages afford, of those affecting considerations which Jesus presented to his disciples, Luke, xii. 22-30, in order to withdraw their minds from the cares and anxieties to which they are so prone to yield during their earthly pilgrimage! Viewing these verses in this light, as *the words of God himself,* can any thing be more adapted to foster the spirit of adoption, or to lead us to cry, Abba, Father? And are they to be expunged from the Sacred Record, as incompatible with the idea we ought to form of inspiration, and unworthy of proceeding from God? But it is at such passages as these that the blind infidel scoffs, while the injudicious or ill-instructed Christian considers them as useless, and converts them into an argument against the plenary inspiration of the Scriptures.

On the same principle that the admonition to Timothy, to drink no longer water, but to use a little wine for the benefit of his health, is rejected as unworthy of verbal inspiration, ought not the truth of the miracle wrought at the marriage at Cana in Galilee, of turning water into wine, to be denied, and the occasion deemed unworthy of miraculous interposition; and especially of its being exhibited as the first of the miracles of Jesus? Shall we be told that *it* also was a " thing not of a religious nature," that it was not worthy to be recorded by the pen of inspiration, that it is not " *prudent*" to speak of such a passage as inspired; or to admit with those, " *if any such there be, who imagine*" that Jesus first manifested forth his glory, by turning a little water into wine?

The levity, not to say the profaneness, of this manner of treating the Holy Scriptures, ought to be held in abhorrence. Their paramount authority, and their unity as the Word of God, are thus set aside. The Bible is converted into another book; and a new revelation, were such licentious principles of interpretation admitted, would become indispensable to teach the humble Christian, who takes it for " a lamp unto his feet, and a light unto his path,"— what portion of it he is to consider as from God, and what portion as from man,—what parts of it are of " a religious nature," from which he may derive edification, and in which he may converse with God, —and what parts relate only to " common or civil affairs," with which he has no concern, and respecting which it would not be *prudent* to speak of them as inspired. If, in this manner, inspiration is first denied to the words, and next to such things as are supposed not to be " of a religious nature," the progress to the non-inspiration of whole books of Scripture, is perfectly easy and natural; and, if whole books are rejected, then both the authenticity and the inspiration of the whole of the Scriptures are subverted. For, if the canon has admitted one uninspired book, there is no security that it has not admitted more; and if that canon has been recognised by Jesus Christ with one uninspired book, every book in the collection may be uninspired, notwithstanding that recognition. If the Apostle Paul has asserted the inspiration of the whole volume, while one book is uninspired, no book in the volume can be received on his authority. The discovery, in like manner, of one single passage in the Scriptures not dictated by the Holy Ghost, would make void the declaration, that " all Scripture is given by inspiration of God," and would render inspiration necessary to tell us what part of it is inspired, and what is not. According to those writers who deny the doctrine of plenary inspiration, we have not the pure Word of God; for much that we have under that designation, is solely the word of man.

Let those who treat the Scriptures in this manner pause, and review the principles on which they are proceeding; and let them cease to perplex " plain Christians" with their rash and unhallowed speculations. The great body of believers receive, with implicit credence, the whole contents of the Bible, as the oracles of God;—they venture neither to add to it nor to take from it. Convinced that it is the book of God, they treat even those parts of it which they do not understand with humble reverence; and in them is fulfilled what is written, Matth. xi. 25, while the fancied wisdom and knowledge of many learned critics has perverted them. Isaiah, xlvii. 10. Those who, in the spirit of little children, read in the Epistles of Paul to Timothy, that " all Scripture is given by inspiration of God," will not easily be induced to believe, that in the very same Epistles the Apostle has contradicted his own declaration, and has afforded at least two examples of the fallacy and unsoundness of what he had, almost in the same breath, so solemnly affirmed. And *it is upon the general ground of these passages being found in Scripture, independently of the meaning which may be affixed to them,* that we denounce the profane manner in which they have been treated, and hold them to be a portion of the Word of God. It was in this light that Origen, who was born towards the end of the second century, viewed those parts of Scripture as inspired, of which he was not able to discover the use. The following are his words, when quoting Mark, x. 50 : " Shall we say that the Evangelist wrote without thought, when he related the man's casting away his garment, and leaping and coming to Jesus? and shall we dare to say that these things were inserted in the Gospels in vain? For my part, I believe that not one jot or tittle of the Divine instruction is in vain.—We are never to say that there is any thing impertinent or superfluous in the Scriptures of the Holy Spirit, though to some they may seem obscure. But we are to turn the eyes of our mind to Him who commanded these things to be written, and seek of Him the interpretation of them. —The sacred Scriptures come from the fulness of the Spirit; so that there is nothing in the Prophets or the Law, or the Gospel, or the Apostles, which descends not from the fulness of the Divine Majesty." "Well knowing," says Irenæus, "that the Scriptures are perfect, as dictated (or spoken) by the Word of God and his Spirit—a heavy punishment awaits those who add to, or take from, the Scriptures."

The inspiration of Luke, in writing the account of Paul's shipwreck, and that of Paul in writing for his cloak, stand upon the same foundation as their inspiration in recording the plan of salvation. But even if it were true, as many ignorantly suppose, that Paul, in his seventh chapter of the first Epistle to the Corinthians, guards against the idea of his inspiration in the cases there referred to, then every thing that he has written, is to be taken as inspired, when he gives no such intimation; and consequently his message about the cloak and parchments, and his medical advice to Timothy, would have their claim to inspiration fully authenticated, even in the view of those persons who pervert the meaning of that chapter.

Some who are satisfied as to the inspiration of all the other parts of the New Testament Scriptures, are doubtful concerning the inspiration of the three books written by Mark and Luke, who were not Apostles. From early accounts concerning these disciples, it is reckoned by many that they were among the seventy whom Jesus sent out in Judea. We know for certain, that they respectively accompanied Peter and Paul in their journeys, and they are mentioned by these two Apostles with much regard. The Apostles not only received the miraculous gifts of the Holy Spirit, but by laying on their hands imparted these gifts to other disciples. When Peter went down to Samaria, he laid his hands on the disciples there, who then received the Holy Ghost. When Paul wrote to the Christians at Rome, he informed them that he longed to see them, that he might impart to them some spiritual gift. Paul had communicated a gift to Timothy whom he employed, as he also did Titus, in directing the churches in his absence. "*I put thee in remembrance, that thou stir up the gift of God which is in thee, by the putting on of my hands.*" By means of these gifts, those who possessed them were enabled to speak in languages they had never learned, and some of them to speak, by " revelation," the mind of God. There can be no reason, then, to doubt, that to Mark and Luke, considering the circumstances in which they stood with the Apostles, the best miraculous gifts were also communicated. They were not Apostles, but they were prophets who received immediate revelations from the Spirit. Eph. iv. 5.

But the conclusive argument as to the inspiration and fitness of these two disciples to contribute the books they have furnished to the sacred volume, does not rest on any supposition, however good the grounds of it may be, but on the fact, that the first churches, *under the immediate guidance and superintendence of the Apostles,* received these books on an equal footing with the other Scriptures. The nation of Israel was appointed by God himself to be the depositaries of the Old Testament Scriptures, which are stamped with the authority of Jesus Christ. In like manner, to that nation which constitutes the kingdom of heaven, the New Testament Scriptures were committed. To it they were addressed and delivered by the Apostles, whom Christ had commissioned to record his words, which these Scriptures contain. The inspiration, therefore, of this second portion of the Holy Scriptures, stands on the same footing with that of the first portion, and is equally stamped with his authority. We appeal to the canon of the Jews with respect to the Old Testament, and we have the same strong ground of confidence, when we receive from the first churches the Scriptures of the New Testament. As, therefore, the Gospels of Mark and Luke, and the Acts of the Apostles, were received by them without dispute, were read by them in their assemblies every Lord's day, and taken for the rule of their duty, as of equal authority with the other Scriptures, which we have already seen by quotations from the early Christian writers; so we conclude with certainty, that these books stand on the same footing in point of authority, in other words, of inspiration, with all the rest, and form a part of the words of Christ, by which we shall be judged at the last day.

Many suppose that the historical parts of Scripture were written by men acquainted with the facts that are recorded, under a Divine *superintendence,* by which they were prevented from falling into any error. This opinion is founded on very low and erroneous ideas of these portions of the Word of God, and of their use. It supposes that these histories are little more than the narrative of the facts they contain, in which we are not greatly concerned. But every fact they record is fraught with important instruction. This idea was so strongly impressed in the Jews, that they maintained that God had more care of the letters and syllables of the Law, than of the stars in heaven; and that upon each title of it, whole mountains of doctrine hung. Hence every individual letter of the Law was numbered by them, and notice was taken how often it occurred. The facts of the Scripture history teach the character of God, and the character of man. They are the history of God's providence and ways, and all of them refer to the work of the Messiah.

The historical parts of Scripture are both introductory to, and illustrative of, the plan of redemption. The general importance, in a religious point of view, of the great outline of the narrations of the Fall,—of the Flood,—of the calling of Abraham, and of the election of the people of Israel,—of their deliverance from Egypt, and their being put in possession of the promised land, must be universally acknowledged. But the whole of the minute detail, by which that outline is filled up, is likewise in the highest degree instructive, and ought to be perused with the most devout attention. The Bible history describes, in action and exhibition, the perfections of Jehovah, as fully as the proclamation in which he declares himself to be long-suffering, and of great mercy, forgiving iniquity and transgression, and by no means clearing the guilty. It delineates the deceitfulness and desperate wickedness of the human heart, as forcibly and distinctly as the annunciations of the prophets, when they " cry aloud and spare not." In the narratives of Scripture, the dependent state, the perverseness, and the folly of man, and the secret motives by which he is actuated, as well as the power, the wisdom, the justice, and the goodness of God in his providential government, and above all in redemption, are vividly depicted. There is not a battle fought by the Israelites, nor a change in the administration of their government, the account of which is not designed for our instruction. There is not an incident recorded as taking place in a private family, that has not a significant meaning.

In the Scriptures there are many things which, considered only in themselves, appear to be of no value, or, at least, of very little importance ; but in reality the Bible contains nothing superfluous—nothing which does not contribute to its perfection, and to the evidence of its divine origin. Besides the list of names in genealogies, we observe many other things in the Word of God, the knowledge of which seems to be of no use ; yet their importance might be proved by numerous examples. We find in the Old Testament several regulations and narrations, which in appearance contribute neither to the strengthening of faith, nor to instruction or consolation. In the book of Moses, matters of the greatest importance are often only touched upon in a few words, while, on the contrary, many things that seem inconsiderable, are dwelt upon at great length. The redemption by the Messiah, which God promised to man immediately after his fall—the calling of the Gentiles predicted to Abraham—the priesthood of Melchisedek, the most illustrious figure of Christ, and many other points of important doctrine, are only noted in a very summary manner. On the other hand, the nativity of Ishmael, the marriage of Isaac, and similar histories, are amply detailed, even in the most minute particulars, but all of them are full of instruction. The single account of Hagar and Ishmael, as interpreted by the Apostle Paul, even to the most inconsiderable circumstance, shows us how we ought to judge of other histories of the Old Testament, although we do not perceive their object. If Abraham had two sons, the one by a bondmaid, the other by a free women, and if the former was cast out of the family; these are the two covenants, the one superseding the other. In that important part of Holy Writ, the eleventh chapter of the Epistle to the Romans, the Apostle Paul unfolds " the deep things of God, which God had revealed to him by his Spirit." How much instruction does he there deduce from the historical fact, that Isaac had two sons, born of the same mother, and at the same time, concerning whom it was said, " *The elder shall serve the younger ;*" which contains a practical exhibition of the great and fundamental doctrines of the PRESCIENCE, the PROVIDENCE, and the SOVEREIGNTY of God, of his PREDESTINATION, ELECTION, and REPROBATION.

Various particulars, apparently of little consequence,

which the Scriptures relate at great length, prove in what way effects the most wonderful have proceeded from causes in themselves inconsiderable; for instance, the birthright of Jacob. God is pleased to teach great things, by things that are small. The prohibitions to take the dam with its young ones in the nest, and not to muzzle the ox that treadeth out the corn, extend farther than at first appears. The act of Jesus Christ in stretching out his hand to touch the leper, does not seem of any account, except to those who know the law which declares that it occasioned uncleanness. The same law forbade the High Priest, who represented Jesus Christ, to enter any house in which there was a dead body. Notwithstanding this, the Lord even touched a bier. In all these particulars, there is a fulness of important doctrine.

Each passage in Scripture has its particular end in view, as the signification of the burning bush, and of the animals described in Ezekiel's vision. The Revelation of John does not present Jesus Christ to all the churches under the same figure. To one it presents the stars and the golden candlesticks. To another, it exhibits the two-edged sword. To another, the eyes like a flame of fire, and feet like fine brass. His titles are according to the diversity of the subjects. Many know, in general, that the ordinances of the ceremonial law prefigured Christ, but are ignorant how, and in what character, each of them represent him. There are none of them which have not an end and particular reason. There are many who, not being acquainted with what the Scripture has in view, are astonished at the recital of different enormities which it particularizes so carefully. The incest of Judah with the wife of his son, might seem as if it should rather have been buried with him, than inserted in the Sacred History, with so many shameful circumstances. Yet if the arrogance of the Jews is considered, who glory in their extraction, and who even found their election as a nation and covenant upon the virtues of their ancestors, we shall see that their errors could not be better refuted, nor their pride more effectually humbled, than by holding up to their view the deeply culpable conduct of their progenitor. The sins of Abraham, of Isaac, and of Jacob, being recorded, was calculated to warn Israel not to seek salvation by the works of the law. The omission of the genealogy of Melchisedek, of his birth, and of his death, denoting the eternity of Jesus Christ, proves how much even the silence of the Scripture is instructive. Every distinct fact recorded in Scripture history may truly be considered an article of faith; for in the plan of Salvation, matters of fact are become doctrines, and doctrines are in the nature of matters of fact. That Jesus Christ was born of a virgin, suffered, and rose again, are all at the same time matters of fact and doctrines. Every fact points to that great event upon which the salvation of man depends—the coming of the Son of God in the likeness of sinful flesh, to redeem a peculiar people to himself—or in some way illustrates his salvation.

In the tenth chapter of the first Epistle to the Corinthians, the essential importance of the historical parts of the Old Testament Scriptures is placed beyond all doubt. After referring to the recorded history of Israel, concerning their passage through the Red Sea, and the manner in which they were conducted in the wilderness, the Apostle adds, "*Now all these things happened to them for examples, and they are written for our admonition, upon whom the ends of the world are come.*" Here the purpose and value of the historical parts of Scripture are demonstrated. They are intended for the *admonition* of the people of God. "*Whatsoever things were written aforetime, were written for our learning, that we through patience and comfort of the Scriptures might have hope.*" Rom. xv. 4. In this passage it is expressly affirmed, that every part of the Old Testament Scriptures was written for the use and edification of believers. Where, then, is there a place for the impious sentiment which some have ventured to promulgate—so derogatory to every idea that we ought to entertain of the oracles of God—so diametrically opposed to all they inculcate respecting their own Divine origin and inspiration, that they contain certain things that are "not of a religious nature," and that "no inspiration was necessary concerning them?" In opposition to such daring and profane theories, Paul, the commissioned and accredited ambassador of Jesus Christ, affirms that "*ALL Scripture is given by inspiration of God, and is profitable for doctrine, for reproof, for correction, for instruction in righteousness, that the man of God may be perfect, thoroughly furnished unto all good works.*"

The above comprehensive declarations include the historical as well as the prophetical and doctrinal parts of the Sacred Oracles, in short, the whole of them.

The object, therefore, of the historical records in the Scriptures, is essentially different from that of all other histories. They are not given to preserve the memory of certain occurrences, in order to promote the knowledge of what may be useful in regard to the affairs of this world, and to extend the sphere of human intelligence and experience; but exclusively to teach the knowledge of God and salvation. Scripture history is conducted in such a manner, that, like the doctrinal parts of the Bible, it is foolishness to the men of the world. It not only disappoints them in the nature of the facts which it relates, but also in the manner in which they are exhibited. Owing to the truth and impartiality of its narrations, the character of the people of Israel appears to them greatly worse than that of the grossest idolaters, and the accounts given in Scripture of men whose conduct on the whole stands approved by God, seems to them to sink below that standard of moral rectitude, to which they imagine that they themselves, and many who make no pretensions to religion, have attained. It not only records truth, without the smallest mixture of error, but also invariably keeps in view the agency of God in every occurrence,—in events the most minute, as well as the most considerable; and thus it furnishes a perpetual comment on the sublime description of the Apostle, when, penetrated with admiration of the riches, both of the wisdom and knowledge of God, he exclaims, " Of Him, and through Him, and to Him, are all things; to whom be glory for ever. Amen."

When the typical import of so many of the sacred narrations, concerning persons, places, institutions, and events, with their necessary bearings, in subserviency to the ushering in of the Messiah, are duly attended to, all may be convinced, that for selecting and relating these histories, in which nothing was to be deficient, and nothing redundant, and for placing before us these mystic pictures for our instruction, the most plenary inspiration, the most accurate divine dictation, was indispensable. The prophets, and even the angels, had but a partial understanding of the things that were afterwards to take place. Moses, it is evident, was not aware, that, as being a type of Christ, it was necessary that his death should intervene, before the people of Israel should be led into the promised land. We have no reason to believe that he understood the import of all he wrote;—for instance, that when he recorded the history of Sarah and Hagar, he knew the design for which it was recorded, and the use that was afterwards to be made of it. We cannot doubt that the prayer of David, " *Open thou mine eyes, that I may see wondrous things out of thy law,*" was equally suitable for Moses, who wrote that law. It was *the Lord* who made the statutes, and judgments, and laws, between him and the children of Israel, *by the hand of* Moses.—Lev. xxvi. 46.

Had the wisest and best informed of the Scripture historians not been inspired of God, but simply superintended, so as to prevent them from falling into error, the histories recorded by them would have been very unlike those which they have actually transmitted. Many of their narrations that exist would never have appeared, and others of them would have been very differently modified. We might have discovered in them the self-approving wisdom of man, but not the seeming " foolishness of God." Would the united sagacity of all the wise men in the world have led them to relate the history of the creation of the universe in one chapter of a book, as Moses has done, and of the erection of the tabernacle in thirteen ? * Would the fond prejudices of the Jewish nation, or the general desire fostered by so many of the learned, to support what is called the dignity of human nature,

---

* If we compare the first chapter of Genesis with the last sixteen of Exodus, excepting the thirty-second and the two following, we shall find a great difference between Moses' describing the construction of the universe and that of the tabernacle. In the one, he is very general and succinct; in the other, he is very copious, and marks the smallest peculiarities. The description of the great edifice of the world seemed truly to require more words than that of a small tent. But, on the contrary, the Spirit of God having presented a short representation of the whole mass of the world, details at great length the structure of the tabernacle. The world was solely constructed for the Church, in order that in it God should be served, and by it his glory manifested, Eph. iii. 10. The tabernacle was, in one view, a figure of the Church. God, thus purposing to show that his church, in which he was to be served, was more precious to him, and more important, than all the rest of the world, has spoken of the tabernacle more amply and more particularly than of all the elements and all the universe together.

in both which Moses no doubt participated, have permitted him to record so base an action as the selling of their brother Joseph as a slave by the Jewish patriarchs,—the incest of Judah, whose tribe was to be always pre-eminent,—and the treachery and revenge of Levi, from whom was to descend the whole priesthood of Israel?

That there was a higher hand which directed the pens of Moses, and of the other writers of sacred history, may be sufficiently manifest to all who have seen in what that history has issued. There is, besides, a combination and a harmony in the historical parts, both of the Old and New Testaments, which we have sufficient ground to believe in a great measure escaped the notice of the writers, as has also been the case with thousands of those who have read them—a variety and a unity which irresistibly prove that *One* only—He who knows the end from the beginning—is the author of the whole, who employed various individuals to produce a uniform work, of which none of them either comprehended all that he contributed to it, or knew for what reason he was directed to record one thing,* and to omit another.

---

* A remarkable instance of this occurs in the repetition of the tenth commandment in the book of Deuteronomy. The Romanists are in the habit of striking out the second commandment, which condemns their idolatry; and, to preserve the appearance of integrity for the decalogue, they divide the tenth commandment into two. The transposition of the two first clauses of this commandment in the book of Deuteronomy, for which at first sight no reason can be assigned, completely stultifies and exposes their artifice.

Considering the purpose which the historical parts of the Scriptures were intended to serve, in exhibiting the character and power of God, and his uninterrupted agency in the government of the world, and in pointing to Him who is the end of the law, we have sufficient reason to be convinced, that neither Moses, nor the other sacred historians, nor all the angels in heaven, though acquainted with all the facts, and under the direction, and with the aid, both of superintendence and elevation, were competent to write the historical parts of the Word of God. They possessed neither foresight nor wisdom sufficient for the work. In both respects, every creature is limited. Into these things, the angels, so far from being qualified to select and indite them, " desire to look," and, from the contemplation of them, derive more knowledge of God than they before possessed, and have their joy even in heaven increased. In those histories, the thoughts and secret motives of men are often unfolded and referred to. Was any one but the Searcher of Hearts competent to this? Could angels have revealed them, unless distinctly made known to them? If it be replied, that in such places the sacred writers enjoyed the inspiration of suggestion, that is, of verbal dictation, we ask, where is the distinction to be found? It is a distinction unknown to the Scriptures. And so far from a plenary inspiration not being necessary in its historical parts, there is not any portion of the sacred volume in which it is more indispensable. But even admitting that verbal inspiration was not in our view essential in those parts of the book of God, is this a reason why we should not receive the testimony of the sacred writers, who nowhere give the most distant hint that they are written under a different kind or degree of inspiration from the rest of it; but who, in the most unqualified manner, assert that full inspiration belongs to the whole of the Scriptures?

The *words* that are used in the prophetical parts of Scripture, must *necessarily* have been communicated to the prophets. They did not always comprehend the meaning of their own predictions, into which they " searched diligently." And in this case, it was impossible that, unless the words had been dictated to them, they could have written intelligibly. Although they had indited the Scriptures, it was necessary to show them "that which is noted in Scripture of truth," Dan. x. 21. The writings of the prophets constitute a great portion of the Old Testament Scriptures, and God claims it as his sole prerogative, to know the things that are to come. We are therefore certain that *they* enjoyed *verbal* inspiration; and, as we have not any where a hint of different kinds of inspiration by which the Scriptures are written, does it not discover the most presumptuous arrogance to assert that there are different kinds?

The nature of the mission of the prophets required the full inspiration which they affirm that they possessed. God never intrusted to any man such a work as they had to perform, nor any part of such a work. It was God himself, " who, at sundry times, and in divers manners, *spake* in time past unto the fathers, *by* the prophets." That work, through which was to be made known " to principalities and powers in heavenly places, the manifold wisdom of God, according to the eternal purpose which he purposed in Christ Jesus," was not a work to be intrusted to any creature. The prophet Micah, iii. 8, says, "*But truly I am full of power by the Spirit of the Lord, and of judgment, and of might, to declare unto Jacob his transgression, and to Israel his sin.*" It was not the prophets then who spoke, but the Spirit of God who spoke by them.

Of the complete direction necessary for such a service as was committed to him, both of lawgiver and prophet, Moses was aware, when the Lord commanded him to go to Pharaoh, and to lead forth the children of Israel from Egypt. In that work he intreated that he might not be employed. This proved the proper sense he entertained of his own unfitness for it. But it was highly sinful, and evinced great weakness of faith, thus to hesitate, after the Lord had informed him that he would be " with him." Moses was accordingly reproved for this, but the ground of his plea was admitted; and full inspiration, not only as to the subject of his mission, but as to the very words he was to employ, was promised. In answer to his objection, the Lord said unto him, Exod. iv. 11, 12, " Who hath made man's mouth? or who maketh the dumb, or deaf, or the seeing, or the blind? have not I the Lord? Now therefore go, and *I will be with thy mouth, and teach thee what thou wilt say.*" Moses still urged his objection, and the same reply was in substance repeated, both in regard to himself and to Aaron. The full inspiration, then, which was at first promised to Moses in general terms, was, for his encouragement, made known in this particular manner, and the promise was distinctly fulfilled. Accordingly, when, as the lawgiver of Israel, he afterwards addressed the people, he was warranted to preface what he enjoined upon them with, " *Thus saith the Lord,*" or, " *These are the words which the Lord hath commanded, that ye should do them.*" In observing all the commandments that Moses commanded them, and in remembering the way by which the Lord had led them, Israel was to learn, that " man doth not live by bread alone, but by every *word* that *proceedeth out of the mouth of the Lord.*" Signs were shown to Moses, and God came unto him in a thick cloud, in order, as he said, " *that the people may hear thee when I speak with thee, and believe thee for ever.*" Exod. xix. 9.

If the words of Moses had not been the words of God,—had he not been conscious of the full verbal inspiration by which he wrote, would the following language have been suitable to him, or would he have ventured to use it? Deuteronomy, iv. 2 : " *Ye shall not add unto the word which I command you, neither shall ye diminish aught from it, that ye may keep these commandments of the Lord your God which I command you.*" Deut. vi. 6 : " *And these words, which I command thee this day, shall be in thine heart; and thou shalt teach them diligently unto thy children.*" Deut. xi. 18 : " *Therefore shall ye lay up these my words in your heart and in your soul, and bind them for a sign upon your head that they may be as frontlets between your eyes. And ye shall teach them to your children, speaking of them when thou sittest in thine house, and when thou walkest by the way, when thou liest down, and when thou risest up. And thou shalt write them upon the door-posts of thine house, and upon thy gates."* From these passages, we learn that Moses was conscious that all the words which he spoke to the people were the words of God. He knew that it was with him as with Balaam, to whom the Lord said, Numbers, xxii. 35, 38, " *Only the word that I shall speak unto thee, that thou shalt speak;*" and in the language of Balaam, Moses could answer, " *The word that God putteth in my mouth, that shall I speak.*"

As " the word of the Lord," was communicated to Moses, so it also came to Gad, to Nathan, and to the other prophets, who were men of God, and in whose mouths was the word of God. " *Now by this I know that thou art a man of God, and that the word of the Lord in thy mouth is truth,*" 1 Kings, xvii. 24. The manner in which the prophets delivered their messages, proves that they considered the words which they wrote, not as their own words, but dictated to them by God himself. Elija said to Ahab, " *Behold I will bring evil upon thee, and will take away thy posterity.*" On this Mr Scott, in his Commentary, observes, " Elija was the voice, the Lord was the speaker, whose words these evidently are." This is a just account of all the messages of the prophets. They introduce them with, " *Thus saith the Lord,*" and declare them to be " *the word of the Lord;*" and is it possible that the prophets could have more explicitly affirmed, that the words which they uttered were communicated to them, and that they were only the instruments of this communication to those whom they addressed? In the place where we read, " Now these be the last words of David, the sweet psalmist of Israel," David says, " *The Spirit of the Lord spake by me, and his word was in my tongue,*" 2 Samuel, xxiii. 2. In like manner it is said, " *And he did that which was evil in the sight of the Lord his God, and humbled not himself before Jeremiah the prophet speaking from the mouth of the Lord,*" " *To fulfil the word of the Lord by the mouth of Jeremiah,*" " *That the word of the Lord spoken by the mouth of Jeremiah might be accomplished,*" 2 Chron. xxxvi. 12, 21, 22. " *Yet many years didst thou forbear them, and testifiedst against them by thy Spirit in the prophets,*" Nehemiah, ix. 30. Isaiah commences his prophecies by summoning the heavens and the earth to hear, " *for the Lord hath spoken,*" Isa. i. 2. In the same manner, Jeremiah writes, " *The words of Jeremiah, to whom the word of the Lord came.*" " *Then the Lord put forth his hand and touched my mouth; and the Lord said unto me, Behold I have put my words in thy mouth.*" " *I will make my words in thy mouth fire,*" Jeremiah, i. 1, 2, 9; v. 14. " *Thus speaketh the Lord God of Israel, saying, Write thee all the words that I have spoken unto thee in a book.*" Jeremiah, xxx. 2. Again, in the prophecies of Ezekiel, " *Son of man, go, get thee unto the house of Israel, and speak my words unto them.*" " *Moreover, he said unto me, Son of man, all my words that I shall speak unto thee, receive in thine heart, and hear with thine ears, and go get thee to them of the captivity, unto the children of thy people, and speak unto them and tell them, Thus saith the Lord God."* Ezekiel, iii. 4, 10, 11. Hosea says, *" The word of the Lord that came unto Hosea;" " The beginning of the word of the Lord by Hosea."* i. 1, 2. It is in similar language that the other prophets generally introduce their predictions, which are every where interspersed with *" thus saith the Lord."*

All, then, that was spoken by the prophets in these several recorded passages, was spoken *in the name of the Lord*. When false prophets appeared, it was necessary for them to profess to speak in the name of the Lord, and to steal his *words* from their neighbour. *" I have heard what the prophets say, that prophesy lies in my name, saying, I have dreamed, I have dreamed. The prophet that hath a dream, let him tell a dream; and he that hath my word, let him speak my word faithfully. What is the chaff to the wheat? saith the Lord. Is not my word like as a fire? saith the Lord; and like a hammer that breaketh the rock in pieces? Therefore, behold, I am against the prophets, saith the Lord, that steal my words every one from his neighbour. Behold, I am against the prophets, saith the Lord, that use their tongues, and say, He saith,"* Jeremiah, xxiii. 25–31. They were the *words* of God, therefore, which the false prophets stole from the true prophets of Jehovah.

The uniform language of Jesus Christ, and his Apostles, respecting the whole of the Old Testament Scriptures, proves that, without exception, they are *" the Word of God."* On what principle but that of the verbal inspiration of Scripture, can we explain our Lord's words, John, x. 35, "*The Scripture cannot be broken?*" Here the argument is founded on one word, " gods," which without verbal inspiration might not have been used; and if used improperly, might have led to idolatry. In proof of the folly of their charge of blasphemy, he refers the Jews to where it is written in their law, " I said ye are gods." The reply to this argument was obvious:—The Psalmist, they might answer, uses the word in a sense that is not proper. But Jesus precluded this observation, by affirming, that " the Scripture cannot be broken," that is, not a word of it can be altered, because it is the Word of Him with whom there is no variableness. Could this be said if the choice of words had been left to men? Here, then, we find our Lord laying down a principle, which for ever sets the question at rest. The Apostles, in like manner, reason from the use of a particular word. Of this we have examples, 1 Corinthians, xv. 27, 28, and Hebrews, ii. 8, where the interpretation of the passages referred to depends on the word " *all.*" Again, Galatians, iii. 16, a most important conclusion is drawn from the use of the word, " *seed,*" in the singular, and not in the plural number. A similar instance occurs, Hebrews, xii. 27, in the expression " *once more,*" quoted from the prophet Haggai.

When the Pharisees came to Jesus, and desired an answer respecting divorce, he replied, " Have ye not read, that *he which made them* at the beginning, made them a male and female; *and said,* for this cause," &c. Thus, what is said in the history by Moses, at the formation of Eve, is appealed to as spoken by God, and as having the authority of a law. But nothing that Moses could say, unless dictated by God, could have the force of a law, to be quoted by our Lord. What, therefore, was then uttered by man, was the Word of God himself.

The Lord Jesus Christ constantly refers to the whole of the Old Testament, as being, in the most minute particulars, of infallible authority. He speaks of the necessity of every word of the Law and the Prophets being fulfilled. " Till heaven and earth pass, *one jot* or *one tittle* shall in no wise pass from the Law, till all be *fulfilled*."—" It is easier for heaven and earth to pass, than *one tittle* of the Law to fail."—But how then shall the Scriptures be *fulfilled?*—That all things which are written may be *fulfilled.*—That the word might be *fulfilled* that is written in their Law.—That the Scripture might be *fulfilled.*—" The Scriptures," he says, " *must be fulfilled.*" In numerous passages the Lord refers to what is " *written*" in the Scriptures, as of equal authority with his own declarations; and, therefore, the words which they contain *must* be the " words of God."

The Apostles use similar language in their many references to the Old Testament Scriptures, which they quote as of decisive authority, and speak of them in the same way as they do of their own writings. " *That ye may be mindful of the words which were spoken before by the holy prophets, and of the commandment of us the Apostles of the Lord and Saviour,*" 2 Peter, iii. 2. Paul says to Timothy, " *From a child thou hast known the Holy Scrip-*

tures, *which are able to make thee wise unto salvation, through faith, which is in Christ Jesus,"* 2 Tim. iii. 15. In this way he proves the importance of the Old Testament Scriptures, and the connexion between the Mosaic and Christian dispensations. The Apostles call the Scriptures " *the oracles of God,"* Rom. iii. 2. What God says is ascribed by them to the Scriptures: " *The Scripture saith unto Pharaoh, Even for this same purpose have I raised thee up, that I might show my power in thee."*—" *For what saith the Scripture? Abraham believed God, and it was counted unto him for righteousness."* " *What saith the Scripture? Cast out the bondwoman and her son."* So much is the Word of God identified with himself, that the Scripture is represented as possessing and exercising the peculiar prerogatives of God: " *The Scripture, foreseeing that God would justify the Heathen;"*—" *The Scripture hath concluded all under sin."*

From the following passages, among others that might be adduced, we learn the true nature of that inspiration which is ascribed to the Old Testament by the writers of the New: Matth. i. 22, " Now all this was done, that it might be fulfilled which was *spoken of the Lord* by the Prophet." Matth. ii. 15, " And was there until the death of Herod: that it might be fulfilled which was *spoken of the Lord* by the Prophet, saying, Out of Egypt have I called my son." Matth. xxii. 43. " He saith unto them, How then doth David, *in spirit,* call him Lord?" Mark, xii. 36, " For David himself said *by the Holy Ghost."* Luke, i. 70, " As he *spake* by the mouth of his

Holy Prophets, which have been since the world began." Acts, i. 16, " Which the *Holy Ghost spoke* by the mouth of David." Acts, xiii. 35, " *He* (God) *saith also* in another Psalm, Thou shalt not suffer thine Holy One to see corruption." These words are here quoted as the words of God, although addressed to himself. In the parallel passage, Acts, ii. 31, the same words are ascribed to David, by whose " mouth" therefore God spoke. Acts, xxviii. 25, " And when they agreed not among themselves, they departed, after that Paul had spoken one word: Well *spake the Holy Ghost* by Esaias the prophet, unto our fathers." Rom. i. 2, " Which *He* had promised afore by his prophets in the Holy Scriptures." Rom. ix. 25, " As *He saith* also in Osee, I will call them my people, which were not my people; and her Beloved, which was not beloved." 1 Cor. vi. 16, 17, " What! know ye not, that he which is joined to an harlot is one body? for two, *saith He*, shall be one flesh." Here the words of Moses are referred to by the Apostle, as they had been by the Lord Jesus Christ himself, as the words of God. Eph. iv. 8, " Wherefore *He saith*, when he ascended up on high." Heb. i. 7, 8, " And of the angels *He saith;*"—" But unto the Son *He saith*." In these passages what was said by the Psalmist, is quoted as said by God. Heb. iii. 7, " Wherefore, as *the Holy Ghost saith*, To-day if ye will hear his voice." Heb. x. 15, " Whereof the Holy Ghost also is a *witness* to us, for after that *He* had *said*." 1 Peter, i. 11, " Searching what, or what manner of time, the Spirit of Christ which was in them did signify, when *He testified* beforehand the sufferings of Christ, and the glory that should follow." And how was it possible that the Prophets could find language in which to express intelligibly the mysteries of God, which they so imperfectly comprehended, unless the Spirit of Christ which was in them had dictated every word they wrote? 2 Peter, i. 20, 21, " Knowing this first, that no prophecy of the Scripture is of any private interpretation, for the prophecy came not in old time by the will of man, but holy men of God *spake as they were moved* by the Holy Ghost."* In this passage the Apostle Peter, having, in the preceding verse, directed the attention of those to whom he wrote, to the " sure word of prophecy," has given an equally comprehensive and explicit attestation to the verbal inspiration of all the prophetic testimony, which comprises so large a portion of the Old Testament, as the Apostle Paul has given, 2 Tim. iii. 16, to that of the whole of the Scriptures, Acts, iv. 25, " *Who by the mouth of thy servant David hast said*, Why did the Heathen rage?" Heb. i. 1, " God, who at sundry times, and in diverse manners, *spake* in time past unto the fathers by the prophets, hath in these last days *spoken* unto us by his Son." The words, then, spoken by the Prophets, were as much the *words of God*, as the words which were spoken by the Lord Jesus Christ himself. And on various occasions Jesus declares, that the words which he spoke were the *words of Him* that sent him.

---

* For the meaning of the expression " private interpretation, see Appendix, No. I.

John viii. 26, 28, "*I speak to the world those things which I have heard of him;*"—"*As my Father hath taught me, I speak these things.*" John, xii. 49, 50, "*I have not spoken of myself, but the Father which sent me, he gave me a commandment what I should say, and what I should speak;*"—"*Whatsoever I speak, therefore, even as the Father said unto me, so I speak.*" John, xiv. 10, "*The words that I speak unto you, I speak not of myself.*" John, xvii. 8, "*I have given unto them the words which thou gavest me.*" John xvii. 14, "*I have given them thy word.*" And this was in strict conformity with what God had declared by Moses, concerning the divine mission of his Son. Deut. xviii. 18, " I will raise them up a Prophet from among their brethren like unto thee, and *will put my words in his mouth;* and he shall speak unto them all that I shall command him. And it shall come to pass, that whosoever will not hearken unto *my words which he shall speak in my name*, I will require it of him."—" He hath made *my mouth*," saith the Redeemer, " like a sharp sword," Isaiah, xlix. 2. " And out of *his mouth* went a sharp two-edged sword," Rev. 1. 16. And again, God saith to the Messiah, " I have put *my words* in thy mouth," Isaiah, li. 16. " And *my words*, which I have put in thy mouth, shall not depart out of thy mouth," Isaiah, lix. 21. The words, then, of which the whole of the Scriptures are composed, are the words *dictated* by God, and *written* by men. Sometimes they are quoted as the words of God, and sometimes as the words of the writers, which proves that in fact they are both. Those who deny that, in some instances, the words used by the penmen of Scripture are the words of God, expressly contradict the assertion of the Apostle, that *All* Scripture is given by inspiration of God, and also disregard the direct testimony of all those passages that have been quoted above, as well as of a multitude of others to the same effect, that are contained in the Scriptures.

The perfect inspiration which belongs to the *Apostles* may be learned from the nature of that SERVICE to which they were appointed, and from the PROMISES which were given to them for the discharge of it, and also from their own DECLARATIONS, the truth of which is attested, not only by the nature of their doctrine, but by the miracles which they wrought.

The commission of the Lord to his Apostles, when he sent them forth in the SERVICE to which he appointed them, was given in these words: Matth. xxviii. 19, 20, " *Go ye, therefore, and teach all nations, baptizing them in the name of the Father, and of the Son, and of the Holy Ghost; teaching them to observe all things whatsoever I have commanded you: and, lo, I am with you alway, even unto the end of the world. Amen.*" Here we see, that the commission of the Apostles included the promulgation of the whole of the doctrine, and of every regulation of the kingdom of God; that it extended to all the world; and that a promise was annexed to it, that the Lord himself would be present with them to the end of time, maintaining and giving efficacy to their testimony, which is recorded in the Scriptures.

This commission is exactly conformable to all that Jesus Christ had at different times said to the Apostles. To Peter, at one time, he declared, Matth. xvi. 19, "*And I will give unto thee the keys of the kingdom of heaven: and whatsoever thou shalt bind on earth shall be bound in heaven: and whatsoever thou shalt loose on earth shall be loosed in heaven.*" Afterwards he repeated this to all the Apostles, Matth. xviii. 18. *Verily I say unto you, whatsoever ye shall bind on earth shall be bound in heaven, and whatsoever ye shall loose on earth shall be loosed in heaven.*" To the same purpose, when he had breathed on them and said, "*Receive ye the Holy Ghost,*" John, xx. 22, he added, "*Whose soever sins ye remit, they are remitted unto them; and whose soever sins ye retain, they are retained.*" In these respects, the Apostles were constituted the authoritative ambassadors of the Lord, and were appointed to an office in which they can have no successors. The laws that, under his authority, they were to establish, and the doctrine they were to promulgate, by which eternal life is conveyed to men, and which are therefore characterised as the keys of the kingdom of heaven, were to be of perpetual and universal obligation. John, xii. 48, "*He that rejecteth me, and receiveth not my words,*" says Jesus, "*hath one that judgeth him. The word that I have spoken,*" (which he had spoken, or was to speak by his Apostles,) "*the same shall judge him in the last day.*" In another place to the same purpose, when speaking of the Apostles having followed him, he says to them, Matth. xix. 28, "*In the regeneration, when the Son of Man shall sit in the throne of his glory, ye also shall sit upon twelve thrones, judging the twelve tribes of Israel."*

The word that the Apostles were to declare, was to open and to shut, and to bind and to loose, in heaven and in earth. It was his own Word, the Word of God, to be uttered by them, by which he would at last judge the world. *" For,"* says he, *" he that receiveth you, receiveth me; and he that receiveth me, receiveth him that sent me,"* Matth. x. 40; which is to the same effect as when he says to the seventy disciples whom he sent out, *" He that heareth you, heareth me: and he that despiseth you, despiseth me; and he that despiseth me, despiseth him that sent me,"* Luke, x. 16. From the awful importance, then, of the service committed to the Apostles, we may judge what kind of inspiration was necessary for those whose *words* were to be the words of the Judge of all. *" We are unto God,"* say they, *" a sweet savour of Christ, in them that are saved and in them that perish. To the one we are the savour of death unto death: and to the other the savour of life unto life: and who is sufficient for these things?"* 2 Cor. ii. 15. The commission of the Apostles embraces every circumstance by which the Divine glory is manifested to every order of intelligent beings—the whole of that revelation of mercy by which the manifold wisdom of God is to be made known to principalities and powers in heavenly places, as well as a complete discovery of the will of God as it regards mankind. Can it be supposed, then, that the heralds of this salvation did not receive a plenary inspiration to qualify them for such a service? That a prophet should be left to the choice of his own words, and be a prophet from God, or that an Apostle should be commissioned to promulgate the laws of the kingdom of Christ, which are everlastingly to bind in heaven and in earth, and yet be permitted to choose for himself the words and language in which these laws should be delivered, is altogether incredible and absurd.* If the words or language are of man's choosing, the Bible becomes partly the book of man and partly the book of God.

The nature of this inspiration, we are also taught by the PROMISES that were given to the Apostles respecting it. When Jesus Christ first sent out his Apostles to proclaim to the house of Israel that his kingdom was at hand, he warned them of the reception they were to meet with, and that they should be brought before governors and kings for his sake. At the same time they were forbidden to use the means which would have been necessary, if in any

---

* " The Apostles, who were divinely commissioned by Christ himself, either were inspired by him with his Spirit, which 'led them into all truth,' or they were *not;* if we say they were not, we make him a liar, for giving them this commission and this promise, as well as them for preaching that they did; and if they *were* thus divinely authorized, it must follow inevitably that what they said was by *him*, and has exactly the same authority as if he had uttered with his own lips. Even an earthly king expects that a messenger sent by him with satisfactory credentials and full powers, should receive the same credit for what he says as would be given to himself in person, and would regard it as an unpardonable affront, if this message so sent were rejected."

measure they had been left to their own judgment. He commanded them to rely entirely upon him, and promised them the inspiration of his Spirit which, in such situations, would be necessary for them: Matth. x. 19, " But when they deliver you up, take no thought how or what ye shall speak; for it shall be given you in that same hour what ye shall speak: For it is *not ye that speak*, but the Spirit of your Father *which speaketh in you.*" Mark, xiii. 11, " But when they shall lead you and deliver you up, take no thought beforehand what ye shall speak, neither do ye premeditate, but whatsoever shall be given you in that hour, that speak ye; *for it is not ye that speak, but the Holy Ghost.*" In the parallel passage, Luke, xii. 12, " For the *Holy Ghost shall teach you* in the same hour *what ye ought to say.*" And again, Luke, xxi. 15, " I will give you a *mouth*, and wisdom which all your adversaries shall not be able to gainsay nor resist." Language cannot more plainly indicate, that the *words* they were to utter, were to be given by inspiration to the Apostles. It was the Holy Spirit who was to speak by them, just as " *God hath* SPOKEN *by the* MOUTH *of all his holy prophets since the world began.*" Acts, iii. 21; Luke, i. 70.

If verbal inspiration was necessary for the Apostles in particular passing circumstances, when they were brought before judges and magistrates; and if, in such occasional situations, as on the day of Pentecost, they actually possessed it, how much more necessary must it have been when they were employed in recording the permanent laws of the kingdom of Christ! It must, therefore, be included in the declarations made by our Lord, in what he says in his last discourse, respecting the Comforter whom he was to send. And that these declarations did refer to the same inspiration, we are not left to conjecture; for we hear the Apostle Paul, when afterwards he addresses a Christian church, asserting that *Christ spake in him,* 2 Cor. xiii. 3. When about to leave his disciples, Jesus said to them, John, xiv. 26, " *But the Comforter, which is the Holy Ghost, whom the Father will send in my name, he shall teach you all things, and bring all things to your remembrance, whatsoever I have said unto you.*" The Apostles were not to trust to their memories, to repeat what Jesus had said to them; but *all* that he had *said* was to be dictated to them by the Holy Ghost. And again, John, xiv. 13, " When he, the Spirit of truth, is come, he will *guide you into all truth;* for he shall not speak of himself, but *whatsoever he shall hear, that shall he speak,* and he will show you things to come." After his resurrection, Jesus Christ said to them, John, xx. 21, " *Peace be unto you; as my Father has sent me, even so send I you.*" His last words to them on earth were these, Acts, i. 8, " *But ye shall receive power after that the Holy Ghost is come upon you, and ye shall be witnesses unto me, both in Jerusalem and in all Judea, and in Samaria, and unto the uttermost parts of the earth.*" Such were the PROMISES given to the Apostles of what they were to receive, to fit them for that great work in which they were about to engage. We shall now hear their own Declarations in respect to their fulfilment.

On the day of Pentecost, Acts, ii. 4, "*They were all filled with the Holy Ghost, and began to speak with other tongues, as the Spirit gave them utterance.*" On that occasion, when speaking in unknown tongues, as was the case with others of the brethren in the churches, 1 Cor. xiv. 13, 28, they *must* have been inspired with every word they spoke, as is asserted in the declaration, that " the Spirit gave them *utterance.*" When, afterwards, having been brought before the Jewish rulers, they had returned to their own company and prayed, Acts, iv. 31, " The place was shaken where they were assembled together, and they were all filled with the Holy Ghost, and they *spake* the *word of God* with boldness." Paul begins his Epistles, by designating himself an *Apostle* of Jesus Christ. Thus he declares his apostolic character and commission from the Lord, by whom he was qualified for his work. We see with what authority he afterwards expresses himself: " *Now unto him that is of power to stablish you according to my gospel, and the preaching of Jesus Christ, according to the revelation of the mystery which was kept secret since the world began; but now is made manifest, and by the Scriptures of the prophets, according to the commandment of the everlasting God, made known to all nations for the obedience of faith.*"— " *Though we,*" says the same Apostle, Galatians, i. 8, " *or an angel from heaven, preach any other gospel unto you than that which we have preached unto you, let him be accursed."*—" *As we said before, so say I now again, If any man preach any other gospel unto you than that ye have received, let him be accursed."*—" *But I certify you, brethren, that the gospel which was preached of me is not after man. For I neither received it of man, neither was I taught it but by the revelation of Jesus Christ."*— 1 Cor. ii. 9, 10, " *But as it is written, eye hath not seen, nor ear heard, neither have entered into the heart of man, the things which God hath prepared for them that love him. But God hath revealed them unto us by his Spirit."*—" *Which things also we speak, not in the words which man's wisdom teacheth, but which the Holy Ghost teacheth,"* 1 Cor. ii. 13. Here, in making a general declaration of what he taught, both the *matter* and the *words* are declared to be from God.* Again he says, 1 Cor. ii. 15, "*For*

---

* On this verse Macknight has the following note:— " *Words taught by the Holy Spirit.*—From this we learn that as often as the Apostles declared the doctrines of the gospel, the Spirit presented these doctrines to their minds clothed in their own language; which indeed is the only way in which the doctrines of the gospel could be presented to their minds. For men are so accustomed to connect ideas with words, that they always think in words. Wherefore, though the language in which the Apostles delivered the doctrines of the gospel, were really suggested to them by the Spirit, it was properly their own style of language. This language in which the doctrines of the gospel was revealed to the Apostles, and in which they delivered these doctrines to the world, is what St Paul calls *the form of sound words,* which Timothy had heard from him, and was to hold fast, 2 Tim. i. 13. Every one, therefore, ought to beware of altering or wrest-

who hath known the mind of the Lord, that he may instruct him? but we have the mind of Christ," 1 Cor. ii. 7, *" We speak the wisdom of God." Eph.* iii. iv, *" Whereby, when ye read, ye may understand my knowledge in the mystery of Christ, which in other ages was not made known unto the sons of men, as it is now revealed unto his holy Apostles and Prophets by the Spirit."* 2 Cor. ii. 10, *" To whom ye forgive any thing, I forgive also ; for if I forgave any thing, to whom I forgave it, for your sakes forgave I it in the person of Christ."* 2 Cor. xiii. 2, 3, " If I come again I will not spare, since you seek a proof *of Christ speaking in me."* In 1 Cor. vii. 17,

---

ing the inspired language of Scripture, in their expositions of the articles of the Christian faith. Taylor, in the sixth chapter of his key, at the end, explains the verse under consideration thus : — *Which things we speak, not in philosophical terms of human invention, but which the Spirit teacheth in the writings of the* Old *Testament:* and contends, that the Apostle's meaning is, that he expressed the Christian privileges in the very same words and phrases, by which the Spirit expressed the privileges of the Jewish church in the writings of the Old Testament. But if the Spirit suggested these words and phrases to the Jewish prophets, why might he not suggest to the Apostles the words and phrases in which they communicated the gospel revelation to the world? Especially as there are many discoveries in the gospel which could not be expressed clearly, if at all, in the words by which the prophets expressed the privilege of the Jewish church. Besides, it is evident, that when the Apostles introduce into their writings the words and phrases of the Jewish prophets, they explain them in other words and phrases, which, no doubt, were suggested to them by the Spirit."

where some have rashly and ignorantly asserted that the Apostle concludes with expressing a doubt whether he was inspired or not, he says, " *so ordain I in all churches.*" Such language, which is precisely similar to that of Moses, Deut. vi. 6, would have been most presumptuous, unless he could have added, as he does a little afterwards, 1 Cor. xiv. 36, " What! came *the word of God* out from you? or came it unto you only? If any man think himself to be a prophet, or spiritual, let him acknowledge that the *things that I write* unto you *are the commandments of the Lord.*" At the opening of the same epistle Paul had said, " *My speech and my preaching was not with enticing words of man's wisdom, but in demonstration of the Spirit and of power.*"—" *We speak the wisdom of God.*" Could any man have used such language unless he had been conscious that he was speaking the words of God? 1 Thess. ii. 13, " For this cause also thank we God, without ceasing, because, when ye received the word of God which ye heard of us, ye received it not as the word of men, but (as it is in truth) *the word of God.*" 1 Thess. iv. 8, " He, therefore, that despiseth, despiseth not *man* but *God*, who hath also given unto us his Holy Spirit." 1 Pet. i. 12, " *Unto whom it was revealed, that not unto themselves, but unto us they did minister the things, which are now reported unto you by them that have preached the gospel unto you with the Holy Ghost sent down from heaven; which things the angels desire to look into.*" 1 Peter i. 23, " *Being born again, not of corruptible seed, but of incorruptible, by the word of God, which liveth and abideth for ever.".* 1 Pet. i. 25, " The *word of the Lord* endureth for ever. And *this is the word* which by the gospel is preached unto you." In referring to the instruction which they gave to the churches, the Apostles characterise it as their " *commandment,*" and refer to it as equivalent to the authority of the Holy Ghost, as in fact it was the same. Acts, xv. 24, 28, " *It seemed good to the Holy Ghost, and to us.*" Such is the inspiration by which all the penmen of the Scriptures wrote, and God has pronounced the most solemn prohibitions against any attempt to add to, or to take from, or to alter, his Word. These warnings are interspersed through every part of the sacred volume; and each of them is equally applicable to the whole of it.

In this manner, that portion of the Scriptures called the *Law* is guarded :—" *Ye shall not add unto the word which I command you, neither shall ye diminish aught from it,*" Deut. iv. 2; xii. 32.

In the next division, sometimes called the *Hagiographa*, it is written, " *Every word of God is pure: He is a shield unto them that put their trust in him. Add thou not unto his words, lest he reprove thee, and thou be found a liar,*" Prov. xxx. 16. The last part of this threatening is infinitely more terrible than the first; for transgressors may be reproved, and yet find mercy, but " all liars shall have their part in the lake which burneth with fire and brimstone, which is the second death," Rev. xxi. 8.

In the prophetical writings, a similar warning is again repeated. They are closed with an intimation, that no more prophets were to be sent, till the fore-

THE HOLY SCRIPTURES. 179

runner of Jehovah (who was to come suddenly to his temple) should appear. Israel is then commanded to regard that revelation which had been made to Moses, concerning Jesus, which the prophets had been commissioned to illustrate, but not to alter; "*Remember ye the law of Moses, my servant, which I commanded unto him in Horeb, for all Israel, with the statutes and judgments,*" Mal. iv. 4.

As, at the conclusion of the Old Testament, where the attention of the people of Israel is called to the first appearance of the Son of God, the Saviour, they are instructed that the prophetic testimony to him is finished; so, at the conclusion of the New Testament, where the attention of all men is directed to his second coming, as the final Judge, the canon of Scripture is closed, and a solemn and most awful warning is given, neither to add to it, nor to take from it: "*I testify unto every man that heareth the words of the prophecy of this book, If any man shall add unto these things, God shall add unto him the plagues that are written in this book; and if any man shall take away from the words of the book of this prophecy, God shall take away his part out of the Book of Life, and out of the Holy City, and from the things which are written in this book,*" Rev. xxii. 18, 19. This passage, so similar to the others above cited, is, for the same reasons for which it is applicable to the book of Revelation, applicable to the whole inspired volume.

In the references that have been made above to many passages of Scripture, to which more of a similar import might have been added, the complete verbal inspiration by which both Prophets and Apostles spoke and wrote, has, by their own DECLARATIONS, been unanswerably established. Whatever they recorded, they recorded by the Spirit of God. Whether they spoke in their own tongue, or in tongues which they had not learned ; or whether they uttered prophecies which they understood, or concerning which they acknowledged, " *I heard, but I understood not,*" Dan. xii. 8; still they spoke or wrote as they were moved by the Holy Ghost. And if we have seen that even the Divine Redeemer himself, *who is over all, God blessed for ever*, when acting in his mediatorial character, as the Father's servant, *spoke*, as he declares, not of himself, but the *words* of Him that sent him ; and that *God the Holy Ghost*, in his office of Comforter, was not to speak of himself, but to *speak* whatsoever he should *hear ;* is it to be presumed that Prophets and Apostles should ever have been left to choose the *words* which they have recorded in the Scriptures?

The words, then, which the Prophets and Apostles recorded, were the *words of God,—Christ spake in them—*they were *the words which the Holy Ghost taught.* The word of God is the sword of the Spirit, Eph. vi. 17. " *It is quick, and powerful, and sharper than any two-edged sword,*" Heb. iv. 12. This *word* was put into the mouths of the Prophets and Apostles ; and therefore their words and commandments have all the authority of the words and commandments of God. " *I stir up your pure minds by way of remembrance, that ye may be mindful of the words which were spoken before by the holy Prophets, and of the commandment of us, the Apostles* *of the Lord and Saviour,*" 2 Pet. iii. 1, 2. The term inspiration loses its meaning when an attempt is made to divide it between God and man. In what an endless perplexity would any man be involved, who was called upon to give to each degree of inspiration, under which it has been supposed the Bible is written, that portion which belongs to it! Let any one undertake the task, and he will soon find that he is building upon the sand. Yet such an attempt should have been made by those daring innovators, be they ancient or modern, who have represented the sacred volume as a motley performance,—part of it written under an inspiration of DIRECTION,—part of it under an inspiration of ELEVATION,—part of it under an inspiration of SUPERINTENDENCE,—(all improperly called inspiration),—and part of it under NO inspiration at all!

But why have such distinctions been introduced? Do they diminish the difficulty of comprehending how the inspiration of the Holy Ghost is communicated to those who are the subjects of it? Is it easier to conceive that a meaning without words should be imparted to the mind of man, than that it should be conveyed to him in words? Instead of being diminished, the difficulty is increased tenfold. But, in either case, we have nothing to do with difficulties; it is a subject which we cannot comprehend; and in whatever way the effect is produced, it is our duty to believe what the Holy Scriptures assert, and not to resort to those vain speculations on the subject by which men darken council by words without knowledge. Every Christian should remember that the view which he takes of the inspiration of the Scriptures is of the greatest practical importance. With what a different feeling must that man read the Bible, who believes that it is a book which partly treats of " common and civil affairs," and partly of " things religious," which is partly the production of God, and partly of men, who were sometimes directed in one way, sometimes in another, and sometimes not directed at all, and that it contains certain things unworthy of being considered as a part of Divine revelation,—from the feeling of the Christian, who reads that sacred book under the solemn conviction that its contents are *wholly* religious, and that *every word* of it is dictated by God! In reading these words, Proverbs, iii. 11, " *My son*, despise not the chastening of the Lord, neither be weary of his correction," how differently must he be affected who reads them as addressed to him merely by Solomon, from the man who views them as addressed to him by his heavenly Father, according to Hebrews, xii. 5! Paul, in that Epistle, in making various quotations from the Old Testament, refers to them expressly as the words of the Holy Ghost. As far as distinctions in inspiration are admitted, their tendency is to diminish our reverence for the Bible, and to exclude as much as possible the agency of the Spirit of God in its composition. In the same way, men eagerly oppose the doctrine of a particular providence, as one on which it is not "*prudent*" to insist, as not "*necessary*," and as " attended *with difficulties*," while they labour to exclude the agency of God from the government of the world, and from the direction of the course of events, by ascribing the whole to the operation of what are called "the laws of nature."

Dr Doddridge, in his Essay on Inspiration, p. 58, after desiring the reader to observe, that in very few instances he has allowed an error in our present copies (of the Scriptures), and that, in these few instances, he has imputed it to translators—adds, " because, as *Mr Seed* very properly expresses it in his excellent *sermon* on this subject, (which, since I wrote the former part of this dissertation, fell into my hands,) *a partial inspiration* is, to all intents and purposes, *no inspiration at all:* For, as he justly argues against the supposition of *any mixture of error* in these *sacred writings,* mankind would be as much embarrassed to know what was *inspired*, and what was *not*, as they could be to *collect a religion* for themselves; the consequence of which would be, that we are left *just where we were*, and that GOD put himself to a great expense of *miracles* to effect nothing at all: a consequence highly derogatory and injurious to his honour." It is not a little remarkable, that such sentiments should be so decisively announced by one who, in the same work, has ascribed various degrees of inspiration to different parts of the Scriptures! Let this glaring inconsistency be considered by those who have followed Dr Doddridge in his unscriptural views on the subject.

It is allowed by Dr Doddridge, that under what is called the inspiration of *suggestion,* " the use of our faculties is superseded, and GOD does as it were *speak directly* to the mind; *making such discoveries to it, as it could not otherwise have obtained, and dictating the very words* in which these discoveries are to be communicated to others; so that a person, in what he writes from hence, is no other than first *the Auditor*, and then, (if I may be allowed the expression,) *the Secretary of* GOD; as *John* was of *our Lord Jesus Christ*, when he wrote from his sacred lips *the seven Epistles to the Asiatic Churches*. And it is no doubt to an *inspiration of this kind* that the Book of the *Revelation* owes its original." (Doddridge on Inspiration, page 41.) Why, then, has Dr Doddridge supposed that any other part of the Bible was written under an inspiration of a different kind? Where did he learn this? Was it less necessary that the Epistles which were written to the other churches, as " the commandments of the Lord," 1 Cor. xiv. 37, should be fully inspired, than for those addressed to the seven churches of Asia? or was it requisite that, to the Book of Revelation, a higher degree of inspiration should belong, than to the other books of the Holy Scriptures? And where, we are entitled to ask, do the Scriptures sanction such distinctions? But if in no part they give to them the smallest countenance, or to any thing similar, what right has any man to introduce distinctions, and to teach what the Scriptures not only have not taught, but the contrary of which they have uniformly and explicitly taught? To invent distinctions that represent some parts of the Scriptures as half inspired, and others not inspired at all, and as relating to things merely civil, is most dishonourable and degrading to the Book of God, and deprives Christians of all that edification which such passages are calculated to afford. Such distinctions, let them be made by whom they may, are the offspring of presumption and folly.

On the whole, we see the nature of that inspiration by which the Prophets and Apostles wrote. The manner of communicating the revelations might differ, Numbers, xii. 6, 7, 8. They might be imparted in a vision, or in a dream, or by speaking mouth to mouth; but their certainty and authority were the same. For the prophecy came not in old time by the will of man, but holy men of God *spake* as they were moved by the Holy Ghost. Neither was it the Apostles who spoke of themselves, but the Spirit of their Father who *spoke* in them, or by them. Let no man, then, venture to introduce distinctions in that inspiration by which the Word of God is written, unheard of in that Word, and therefore totally unwarranted and unauthorized. It is not for men to say, " How can these things be?" No man comprehends himself either in soul or body, nor can we tell how the one acts upon the other: And shall vain man, who " would be wise, though man be born like the wild ass's colt," stumble at, and reject, the declarations of God concerning that inspiration which belongs to his Word, and by which he makes known his pleasure? " The wind bloweth where it listeth, and thou hearest the sound thereof, but canst not tell whence it cometh, and whither it goeth." The Lord is able to communicate his will in whatever way he pleases, although we cannot trace the manner of his operation. In the words spoken by the ass of Balaam, we have an example of this communication, through an unconscious and involuntary instrument.* In Balaam himself we have an example through one who was conscious, but involuntary, in the declaration he made respecting Israel. In Caiaphas, through one who was voluntary in what he said, but unconscious of its import. And in the writers of the Scriptures, we have an example of agents both voluntary and conscious, but equally actuated by the Spirit of God.

The dictating of that Law which is perfect, every jot and tittle of which was to be fulfilled,—of those histories which were written for the " admonition" of all future generations,—of the institutions of that kingdom which is to endure for ever,—and of that Word by which all shall be judged, was, and necessarily must have been, the work of perfect, that is, of infinite wisdom; Psalm xix. 7, " *The law of the Lord is perfect.*"—But if certain parts of it are the words of men, who wrote merely under a superintendence which preserved them from recording what is false or erroneous, these parts must, like their authors, be imperfect. The same would hold true respecting all that is supposed to be written under an inspiration of elevation, which, whatever it may mean, could not be carried beyond that enlargement of which the mind of man is capable. The Bible can only be perfect, if it be the Word of God

---

* Under which of the kinds of inspiration that have been so ingeniously forged, did the ass of Balaam speak? Was it under that of *Elevation?* Or shall the truth of the fact be rejected altogether, because it is " attended with difficulties!"

himself from one end to the other. But, if the words of the writers of it be solely their own words, or be they the words of Angels, Principalities, or Powers, they are imperfect,—and the Bible is an imperfect book.

The perfection of the Scriptures is necessary for the purpose they were intended to serve. " The heavens declare the glory of God; and the firmament showeth his handiwork," Psalm xix. 1. " By the things that are made" God's eternal power and Godhead are clearly seen, so as to render men " without excuse," Rom. i. 20; and there they leave him under condemnation. But " *The law of the Lord is perfect, converting the soul: the testimony of the Lord is sure, making wise the simple. The statutes of the Lord are right, rejoicing the heart: the commandment of the Lord is pure, enlightening the eyes.*"—It is not, then, by the works of creation,—it is not by his dealings towards either holy or fallen angels, that the glory of God is fully displayed. This honour is reserved for the history of the incarnation of his Son. It is here, and only here, that mercy and truth meet together, that righteousness and peace embrace each other;—truth has sprung out of the earth, and righteousness has looked down from heaven. Here justice and judgment are seen to be the habitation of Jehovah's throne,—and mercy and truth to go before his face.

" *Drop down, ye heavens, from above, and let the skies pour down righteousness; let the earth open, and let them bring forth salvation, and let righteousness spring up together; I the Lord have created it,*"

Isaiah, xlv. 8. Here is something far more glorious than all that was ever before seen in the universe of God!—a righteousness exalted to absolute perfection, and rendered infinitely glorious by the union of the divine with the human nature. God charged his Angels with folly, and the heavens are not clean in his sight, but with him who wrought this righteousness, he is " well pleased."

The righteousness of Adam in innocence, or the righteousness of angels in glory, was the righteousness of creatures, and therefore a limited righteousness. It consisted in the love and service of God, which they rendered with all their heart and strength; but further it could not go. Their righteousness was available in the time only while it continued to be performed, and it might cease and be lost. But that righteousness which the skies have poured down, is a righteousness that is infinite, and that shall never be abolished, Isaiah, li. 6, 8. It is a righteousness that was performed in a limited period of time, by Him who is called " JEHOVAH OUR RIGHTEOUSNESS;" but the glory of it was contemplated from eternity, while its efficacy extends back to the fall of man, and forward through all the ages of eternity. It is the " *everlasting righteousness,*" which, as the prophet Daniel predicted, was brought in by the Messiah. It is "*the righteousness of our God and Saviour Jesus Christ,*" 2 Peter, i. 1, of which Noah was a preacher, 2 Pet. ii. 5, and of which he was an heir, Heb. xi. 7, the ministration of which was committed to the Apostles, 2 Cor. iii. 9. It shall be through eternity the delight of the Father, the admiration of angels, and the song of the redeemed.

THE HOLY SCRIPTURES. 189

It is in the Bible that this RIGHTEOUSNESS is made known. In the Bible the Gospel is recorded, which is the power of God unto salvation, *because therein is the* RIGHTEOUSNESS OF GOD *revealed*, Rom. i. 17. The Bible contains the record of the eternal purpose of God, which he purposed in Christ Jesus,—of the unsearchable riches of Christ,—of the eternal election of Him to be the Mediator between God and man, and of the eternal election of his people in Him,—of his incarnation, humiliation, exaltation, and glory. And " in as much as he who hath builded the house hath more honour than the house," insomuch is there a higher display of the glory of God, in the history contained in the Bible, of Him who was " God manifest in the flesh," than is afforded in the creation, and the discovery of all the other works of God in the universe, animate and inanimate, of which Jesus Christ is the Creator and the Head. Hence is that preference justified which is given to the Bible above them all, " *Thou hast magnified thy* WORD *above all thy name*." The earth and the heavens shall perish,—" As a vesture shalt thou fold them up, and they shall be changed,—*But the word of the Lord endureth for ever. And this is the word which by the Gospel is preached unto you.*"

Such, then, is the perfection of the Bible, for the writing of which, the most complete inspiration was absolutely indispensable, in order that it should be entirely the word and the work of God,—in thought, —in meaning,—in style,—in expression,—in every part,—in the strictest sense, the word or voice of God to man. Each part is necessary in its place to complete the whole,—and if any one part were wanting, however inconsiderable it may appear, that absolute perfection, that complete adaptation to the end proposed, which belong to the *Book of God*, would be destroyed.

Christians ought to beware of giving up in the smallest degree the inspiration of the Bible. That precious deposit is now delivered to their keeping, as the first portion of it was committed to the Jews. The Jews were constituted the " witnesses" of Jehovah, Isaiah, xliii. 10, 12 ; until the time arrived, when, in his sovereign pleasure, he appointed other " witnesses," Acts, i. 8. The nation of Israel was his peculiar treasure,—an holy nation, Exodus, xix. 5, 6 ; till, by their final rejection of his Son, they forfeited that title, and he gave his vineyard to other husbandmen, Matth. xxi. 41. They possessed the peculiar "name" which he had conferred on them, till the prophecy concerning it was fulfilled, when it was left " for a curse," Isaiah, lxv. 15 ; and when a new name was bestowed on those who were henceforward to be acknowledged as the people of God, Acts, xi. 26; 1 Peter, iv. 16. Having now become the depositaries of the whole volume of inspiration, let *Christians* regard it with the same unshaken fidelity, with which, before being completed, " *the* WORDS *which the Lord of Hosts hath sent in his Spirit by the former prophets,*" Zechariah, vii. 7, 12, were preserved by the *Jews*. Let them not weaken by vain reasonings, the impression produced upon their minds by the testimony of the Bible itself concerning its full inspiration in every part, nor substitute for it, a book which, in their imagination, is only partially inspired,—which contains sometimes the words of God, and sometimes the words of men who spake not as they were moved by the Holy Ghost, but who were only preserved from error, or who wrote " *as any other plain and faithful men might do.*" By such sentiments, the offspring of philosophy and vain deceit, after the tradition of men, after the rudiments of the world, and not after Christ, has the Bible been degraded, and its high title to the designation of " the oracles of God" made void. In opposition to these heretical opinions, be they ancient or modern, let every disciple of Him whose command it is to " search the Scriptures," regard it as a *faithful* saying, and not liable to doubtful interpretations, that " A<small>LL</small> *Scripture is given by inspiration of God, and is profitable for doctrine, for reproof, for correction, for instruction in righteousness ; that the man of God may be perfect, thoroughly furnished unto all good works.*"

The testimony to the *truth* of the Scriptures, which arises from their inspiration, is of the strongest kind. By presenting themselves as *inspired*, they bring the truth of their contents to the most decisive test. They occupy ground which nothing but *truth* and *perfection* can enable them to maintain. Could there be found in them any thing absurd, or false, or erroneous ; could the smallest flaw in the character or doctrine of the Author of Salvation ; any degree of weakness, of want of wisdom ; or any contradiction be detected, they must immediately be compelled to relinquish this ground. The claim of inspiration is an assertion of the infinite importance, and incomparable excellency of the matter which they contain, as what man, without them, never could have discovered; and also that it is delivered in a style suitable to the dignity of what they present. They contain many chains of prophecies, as well as multitudes of detached predictions, now fulfilling, or that have been fulfilled in different ages ; and they defy the perspicacity of man to falsify a single one of them. They assert a number of facts respecting various particulars of the creation, the age, and the history of the world ; of a general deluge; of the descent of all mankind from a single pair ; of the primeval condition of man, as civilized, and not savage ; of the origin of a variety of universal customs, otherwise unaccountable, as of sacrifice, and of the division of time by weeks. Yet, after all the severest scrutinies of the most enlightened, as well as most inveterate opposers in ancient and modern times, not one fact which they assert has been disproved. On the contrary, these facts are constantly acquiring fresh evidence, from various sources. The consistency, too, of the doctrine of the several writers of Scripture is particularly observable, and forms a striking contrast to the discordant opinions, inconsistencies, and self-contradictions of the Greek and Roman, as well as of modern writers, on almost every subject of which they treat.

Since, then, the Scriptures advance a claim that nothing but their truth could sustain, and which could be so easily disproved, if false; since they are the only writings ever published that could bear such a test, there is the most demonstrative evidence that they are the Word of God. The industry and researches of philosophers have detected error in the noblest productions of ancient wisdom, but all the light of science, throughout all the ages of the world, has not been able to discover one single error in the Bible.

APPENDIX.

No. I. p. 166.

Meaning of the expression—" private interpretation."

Knowing this first, that no prophecy of the Scripture is of any private interpretation, for the prophecy came not in old time by the will of man; but holy men of God spake as they were moved by the Holy Ghost, 2 Peter i. 20, 21. Several commentators have affixed a meaning to the concluding words in the 20th verse which is altogether erroneous. Parkhurst, in his Dictionary, calls it a "difficult passage," and the Roman Catholics have made great use of it to prove that the Scriptures cannot be understood unless explained by what they call the church. The Apostle has, however, himself clearly explained, in the 21st verse, what he intends by the expression " private interpretation." The word translated interpretation, literally signifies the loosing of a knot, or unbinding, that is, unfolding. It is rendered "declaration," in Martin's, and other French translations. The verb from which it is derived, which is precisely of the same import, is translated " expounded," Mark iv. 34, and " determined," Acts xix. 39, meaning, as above, unfolded, declared. " Dr Mill," says Benson, " hath, in a few words, given the sense of this place : ' In writing, the prophet did not interpret, or explain, his own mind ; but the mind and will of the Holy Spirit, with which he was inspired.'" " Prophecy comes not," says Whitby, "from the Prophet's own suggestion, but from the inspiration of the Holy Ghost. That this is the true sense of these words appears from the Apostle's own interpretation;" &c. HENRY observes, "No Scripture prophecy is of private interpretation, or a man's own proper opinion, an explication of his own mind, but the revelation of the mind of God. This was the difference between the prophets of the Lord and the false prophets who have been in the world. The prophets of the Lord did not speak or do any thing of their own mind, as Moses, the chief of them, says expressly, Numb. xvi. 28. *I have not done any of the works* (nor delivered any of the statutes and ordinances) *of my own mind.* But false prophets *speak a vision of their own heart, not out of the mouth of the Lord,* Jer. xxxiii. 16." CALVIN's exposition of these words is as follows:—" S. Pierre entend que l'Ecriture n'a point esté mise en avant par volonté ou mouvement humain. Car nous ne serons jamais bien disposez pour la lire, si nous n'y apportons reverence, obeissance, et docilité. Ou la vraye reverence procede de la, quand nous nous proposons que c'est Dieu qui parle a nous, & non point des hommes mortels. Sainct Pierre donc veut principalement qu'on adjouste foy aux propheties, comme a oracles de Dieu indubitables: d'autant qu'elles ne sont procedées du propre mouvement des hommes. Et a cela tend ce qu'il adjouste incontinent apres, ascavoir que *les saincts hommes de Dieu ont parlé, etans poussez du S. Esprit;* et non point prononcé d'eux mesmes & a leur fantasie quelque inventions de leur cerveau. Brief, il veut dire que le commencement de droite intelligence est, quand nous attribuons aux saincts Prophetes, l'authorité qui est du a Dieu mesmes."

In the commentary of MARETS, first professor in theology in the university of Groningen, we have the following note on the same words, which in his Bible are translated, as in the text of Calvin, "*particuliere declaration,*" which, he observes, signifies " detachement, ou explication: l'Apôtre s'en sert ici, ou pour exprimer l'exposition et la proposition même que les Prophetes ont fait de leur propheties, par laquelle ils n'ont pas mis en avant ni exposé et proposé aux hommes, ce qu'ils trouvoient bon d'eux memes, mais le conseil de Dieu, non pas ce qui procedoit de leur cru par un *mouvement particulier*, (car ou pouroit ainsi traduire ces mots) mais de l'inspiration de l'Esprit de Dieu." On this passage CLAUDE, in his letter to Monsieur C. de Paris, le 27 de Juin 1679, observes, p. 306. " L'Ecriture est la Parole de Dieu, une revelation surnaturelle. *Toute l'Ecriture*, dit Saint Paul, 2 Timothe, iii. 16, *est divinement inspirée*. A quoi se rapoite ce que dit Saint Pierre, 2, chap. i. v. 20, 21, *Que nulle Prophétie de l'Ecriture n'est de particuliere declaration*, c'est a dire, que les Prophétes n'ont pas expliqué les Oracles de l'ancien Testament, de leur propre mouvement, *car la prophétie n'a pas été autrefois apportée par la volonté de l'homme, mais les saints hommes de Dieu ont parlé, poussez par le Saint Esprit.*"

No. II.

The following are Extracts on the Verbal Inspiration of the Scriptures, from the Works of Eminent Christian Writers:

IRENÆUS, who conversed with Polycarp, the disciple of John, and who himself lived but a few years after that Apostle, says, " Well knowing that the Scriptures are *perfect*, as *dictated* (or spoken) by the word of God, and his Spirit,—a heavy punishment awaits those who add to, or take from, the Scriptures. But we follow the one and only true God, as our teacher; and having his *words* as a rule of truth, do always speak the same things concerning the same things."

To the same purpose, ORIGEN, born in the second century, speaks of it as a common opinion, " That the sacred books are not *writings of men*, but have been written and delivered to us from the inspiration of the Holy Spirit, by the will of the Father of all things, through Jesus Christ." And again, " The sacred Scriptures come from the fulness of the Spirit; so that there is nothing in the Prophets, or the Law, or the Gospel, and the

Epistles, which descends not from the Divine Majesty,"—"one and the same Spirit proceeding from the one God, teaching the like things in the Scriptures written before the coming of Christ, and in the Gospels and Apostles." "For my part, I believe that not one jot or tittle of the divine instructions is in vain." "Let us come daily to the wells of the Scriptures, *the waters* of the Holy Spirit, and there draw and carry home a full vessel." Lardner, vol. II. 172, 488, 495.

"It is asked—If in writing, they (the sacred writers) were so acted upon and inspired by the Holy Spirit, both as to the things themselves, and as to the *words*, that they were free from all error, and that their writings are truly authentic and divine? The adversaries deny this. We affirm it."

"Scripture proves itself divine from its style; Divine Majesty shining not less from the simplicity than the gravity of its *diction*."

"Nor can it easily be believed that God, who has dictated and inspired *all and the very words*, to men divinely inspired, has not taken care also about the preservation of them all."*

"But God has instituted the Scripture, partly by *revelation*, which has been accomplished, 1. By *writing*, as was shown in the giving of the Law. 2. By *commanding*, that it might be written, Deut. xxxi. 19. Rev. i. 19, 3. 3. By *inspiring*, 2 Tim. iii. 16, that is, by suggesting the *things that were to be written*, and infallibly directing the *writing* ; so fully, that in all things, whether

---

* Institutio Theologiæ Francisco Turretino, Vol. I. p. 70.—" Quæritur—An in scribendo ita acti et inspirati fuerint a Spiritu Sancto, (scriptores sacri,) et quoad res ipsas, et quoad verba, ut ab omni errore immunes fuerint, et scripta ipsorum vere sint authentica et divina ? Adversarii negant; nos affirmamus."

"Scriptura seipsam divinam probat—ex parte *styli* ; Divina *Majestas*, non minus ex simplicitate quam gravitate dictionis elucens." Page 71.

"Nec facile credi potest, Deum, qui omnia et singula verba viris Θεοπνευϛοις dictavit et inspiravit, de omnibus etiam conservandis non curasse." Page 80.

relating to matters of doctrine or of fact, he not only inspired the things themselves, but has even dictated the *very words*, partly by *canonization*," &c. *

" The Scripture is principally called the Word of God, on account of the infallible inspiration which belongs to it—to the *words* equally as to the things, in which, therefore, nothing irrelevant occurs, although God has wisely accommodated himself to the style of each of the amanuenses in writing, as to the sound of the voice in speaking."†

CALVIN, in his Commentary on 2d Tim. iii. 16, says, " To show the authority (of Scripture) he (Paul) says, that *it is divinely inspired.* For if it be so, without contradiction men ought to receive it with reverence. And this is the principle which distinguishes our religion from all others, namely, that we know that God hath spoken to us, and are fully assured that the Prophets have not spoken from themselves, but as organs and instruments of the Holy Spirit, and that they have solely announced what they had received from on high. Whoever then would profit by the Holy Scriptures, let him first decide this within himself, that the Law and the Prophets are not a doctrine which has been given according to the desire or will of men, but dictated by the Holy Spirit. If any object, how can we know this; the answer is, that God declares and manifests that he is the au-

---

* Theologia, &c. PETRO VAN MASTRICHT, Vol I. p 21. sect. 19.—" Condidit autem Deus scripturam : partim *rerelatione*, quæ peracta est, 1. *Scribendo*, ut in decalogo conspicuum. 2. *Mandando*, ut scriberetur, Deut. xxxi. 19. Apoc. i 19. 3. *Inspirando*, 2. Tim. iii. 16. *h. e.* suggerendo *scribenda*, et infallibiliter dirigendo *sciiptionem.* Usque adeo, ut in omnibus, sive in jure versentur, sive in facto ; non solum res ipsas inspiraverit, sed etiam singula verba dictarit : partim *canonizatione,*" &c.

† JOHANNIS MARCKII Theologiæ Medulla, &c.—" Scriptura *verbum Dei* præcipue dicitur ob *inspirationem infallibilem*, 2 Tim. iii. 16. 2 Pet 1. 20, 21, quæ pertinet—ad *verba* denique æque quam ad res, in quibus proinde nihil inepti occurrit ; etiamsi singulorum Amanuensium stylo prudenter Deus se accommodaverit in scribendo, æque quam vocis sono in loquendo." Page 12 and 13, sect. 5.

thor of it as much to the disciples as to the teachers, by the revelation of that same Spirit. For Moses and the Prophets have not given forth at random what we have as written by them; but inasmuch as they spoke, being impelled (poussez) by God, they have witnessed boldly, and without any fear, that which was true, that it was the mouth of God who had spoken. . . . Observe from the first member, (of this verse,) that the same reverence that we have for God is due also to the Scripture, because it has proceeded from him alone, and has nothing of man mixed with it.*

"The Holy Spirit made use of the pens of the Evangelists, and of the Apostles, for the writings of the New Testament, as he had formerly made use of those of Moses and the Prophets for the Old. He furnished them with the occasions for writing. He gave them the desire, the power to do it. The matter, the form, the order, the economy, the *expressions*, are of his immediate inspiration, and of his direction."†

---

* "Pour monstrer l'authorité, il dit qu'*elle est inspirée Dirinement*. Car si ainsi est, sans aucun contredit les hommes la doyuet recevoir en reverence. Et c'est le principe, qui discerne notre religion de toutes autres, ascavoir que nous scavons que Dieu a parlé a nous, et sommes certainement assemé que les Prophétes n'ont pas parlé de leur propre sens. Mais comme organes et instruments du S. Esprit, qu'ils ont seulement annoncé ce qu'ils avoyent receu d'enhaut. Quiconque donc voudra proufiter ens sainctes Escritures, qu'il arreste premierement ceci en soy mesme, que la Loy et les Prophétes ne sont point vue doctrine qui ait este donnee a l'appetit ou la volonté des hommes, mais dictée par le Sanct Esprit. Si on objecte, d'où c'est qu'on pourra scavoir cela; je respon que Dieu declare et manifeste qu'il est autheur di'celle tant aux disciples qu'au docteurs, par la revelation de ce mesme Esprit. Car Moyse et les Prophétes n'ont point a la volee mis en lumiere ce que nous avons par escrit de leur main, mais d'autant qu'ils parloyent estans poussez de Dieu, ils ont tesmoigne' hardiment et sans aucune crainte ce qui estoit veritable, que c'estoit la bouche de Dieu qui avoit parlé . . . . Voyla le premier membre, que telle reverence que nous portons a Dieu, est deue aussi a l'Escriture, pource qu'elle est procedée de luy seul, et n'ha rien de l'homme mesle avec soy."

† CLAUDE.—Posthumous Works, Vol. IV. p. 228.—"Le Saint Esprit s'est servi de la plume des Evangelistes et des Apôtres pour les ecritures du Nouveau Testament, comme il s'etoit autre fois servi de celles de

"If you understand, that the Prophets and the Apostles have not been instruments purely passive; instruments impelled by inspiration, in all respects: and that, on the contrary, they have been instruments acting by a power which belonged to them, like other second causes, I maintain that it is false. They were no more than simply organs whom the Holy Spirit made use of to write, having done nothing in what respects their part, but formed the letters and the characters of the Scriptures, under the conduct of the same Spirit, for as to all the other things, the Holy Spirit hath himself dictated to them."*

Hooker, in his first sermon on Jude, says, "God, which lightened thus the eyes of their understanding, giving them knowledge by unusual and extraordinary means, did also miraculously himself frame and fashion their words and writings, insomuch that a greater difference there seemeth not to be between the manner of their knowledge, than there is between the manner of their speech and ours. . . . . . But '*God hath made my mouth like a sword,*' saith Isay. And '*we have received,*' saith the Apostle, '*not the Spirit of the world, but the Spirit which is of God, that we might know the things which are given to us of God, which things also we speak, not in words, which man's wisdom teacheth, but which the Holy Ghost doth teach.*' This is that which the Prophets mean by those books written full, within and without;

Moyse et des Prophétes pour l'Ancien. Il leur a fourni les occasions d'ecrire, il leur en a donné le desir et les forces. La matière, la forme, l'ordre, l'œconomie, les expressions sont de son inspiration immediate et de sa direction"

* "Si vous entendez, que les Prophétes et les Apôtres n'ont pas été des instrumens purement passifs; des instrumens poussez par des inspirations, dans toutes les manieres: and qu'au contraire, ils ont été des instrumens agissans par une vertu que leur fût propre, comme sont les autres causes secondes, je soutiens que cela est faux · ils n'ont été, simplement que les organes dont le Saint Esprit s'est servi pour écrire n'ayant pour ce qui les regarde, que formé les lettres et les caractéres de l'Ecriture sous la conduite du meme Esprit, car pour toutes les autres choses, le Saint Esprit les a dictées immediatement lui meme."—Claude's *Letters*, p. 653.

which books were so often delivered them to eat, not because God fed them with ink and paper, but to teach us, that so oft as he employed them in this heavenly work, they neither spake nor wrote any word of their own, but uttered syllable by syllable as the Spirit put it into their mouths, no otherwise than the harp or the lute doth give a sound according to the discretion of his hands that holdeth and striketh it with skill. The difference is only this: An instrument, whether it be a pipe or harp, maketh a distinction in the times and sounds, which distinction is well perceived of the hearer, the instrument itself understanding not what is piped or harped. The Prophets and holy men of God not so. ' *I opened my mouth,*' saith *Ezechiel,* ' and *God reached me a scroul. Son of man, cause thy belly to eat, and fill thy bowels with this I give thee. I eat, and it was sweet in my mouth as honey,*' saith the Prophet. Yea sweeter, I am persuaded, than either honey or the honey comb. For herein they were not like harps or lutes, but they felt, they felt the power and strength of their own words. When they spake of our peace, every corner of their hearts was filled with joy. When they prophesied of mournings, lamentations, and woes to fall upon us, they wept in the bitterness and indignation of spirit, the arm of the Lord being mighty and strong upon them."

In the dedication of Hooker's Sermon of Mr Henry Jackson to Mr George Summaster, Principal of Broad-Gates Hall, in Oxford, the former says, " Sir—Your kind acceptance of a former testification of that respect I owe you, hath made me venture to show the world these Godly Sermons under your name. In which, as every point is worth observation, so some especially are to be noted. The first, that, as the spirit of Prophecy is from God himself, who doth inwardly heat and enlighten the hearts and minds of his holy penmen, (which if some would diligently consider, they would not puzzle themselves with the contentions of *Scott, and Thomas, whether God only, or his ministering spirits, do infuse into men's minds prophetical revelations, per species intelligibiles,*) so God framed their words also. Whence the holy father *St Augustine* religiously observeth, That all those that understand the sacred writers, will also perceive, that they ought not to use other words than they did, in expressing those heavenly mysteries which their hearts *conceived*, as the *Blessed Virgin* did our Saviour, *by the Holy Ghost.*"—Hooker's Works, 1662, pp. 283, 4.

BOYLE, in his " Considerations touching the Style of the Holy Scriptures," *every where* asserts that God is the *author* of the Scriptures, and the writers no more than his secretaries, as page 17. He calls the Holy Ghost " the writer of the Scriptures, and the method of the Scriptures the Holy Ghost's way of writing," p. 56. " The inspired writers had their pens guided by an omniscient hand, and were but the several secretaries of the same enditer," p. 76. " We are not to believe that so divine an enditer, by secretaries," &c., p. 79. " The prophetic spirit that edited them," (the Scriptures,) p. 81. Boyle calls God the author of the Scriptures, p. 122; and next page he calls the Bible " a book published by an omniscient enditer." The Scriptures are " God's dictates," p. 125. " Amongst the thirteen articles of the Jewish creed, one acknowledges the very expressions of the Law, (or Pentateuch,) to have been inspired by God," pp. 128, 129. " He vouchsafes to speak to *us* in almost as glorious a manner as he did to *Moses*," p. 133. And speaking against profaneness, as it relates to the Scriptures, he says, " and perhaps passing to the impudence of perverting inspired expressions," p. 178.

Dr OWEN, in his Exposition of the Epistle to the Hebrews, Exercitation 1, expresses himself as follows. " And thus, not this or that part, but 2 Timothy, iii. 16, all Scripture was given by inspiration. And herein all the parts or books of it are absolutely equal. And in the going out of the whole, 2 Pet. i. 21, holy men of God spake as they were moved by the Holy Ghost. So that whatever different means God at any time might make use of, in the communication of his mind and will unto any of the prophets or penmen of the Scripture, it was this divine inspiration, and being acted by the Holy Ghost both as to things and words, that rendered them infallible revealers of him unto the church. And thus the foundation of the canonical authority of the books of the Scripture, is absolutely the same in and unto them all, without the least variety either from any difference in kind or degree."

Dr Owen, in his book " *Of the Divine Originall, with the authority, self-evidencing power, and light of the Holy Scriptures,*" p. 5, 10, says, " The various ways of special Revelation, by *Dreams, Visions, Audible Voices, Inspirations,* with that peculiar one of the *Law-giver,* under the Old Testament, called *face to face,* Exod. xxxiii. 11, Deut. xxxiv. 10, and Numbers, xi. 8, with that which is compared with it, and exalted above it, (Heb. i. 1, 2, 3,) in the *New,* by the *Son, from the bosom of the Father,* John, i. 17, 18, are not of my present consideration, all of them belonging to the *manner* of the thing inquired after, not the *thing* itself.

"By the assertion then laid down of God *speaking in the prophets of old,* from the beginning to the end of that long tract of time, consisting of 1000 years, wherein he gave out the writings of the Old Testament; two things are ascertained unto us, which are the *foundation* of our present discourse.

" 1. That the *Laws* they made known, the *Doctrines* they delivered, the *Instructions* they gave, the *Stories* they recorded, the *Promises* of Christ, the *Prophecies* of Gospel times they gave out, and revealed, were not their own, not conceived in their *Minds,* not formed by their *Reasonings,* not retained in their *Memories* from what they had heard, not by any means beforehand comprehended by them, (1 Pet. i. 10, 11,) but were all of them *immediately* from God; there being only a passive concurrence of their rational faculties in their reception, without any such *active obedience,* as by any Law they might be obliged unto Hence, 2dly, God was so *with* them, and by the Holy Ghost so *spake in them,* as to their *receiving* of the *word* from him, and their delivering of it unto others by *speaking* or writing, as that they were not themselves enabled by any *habitual light,* knowledge or conviction of Truth, to declare his Mind and Will, but only *acted* as they were immediately *moved* by him. Their

Tongue in what they said, or their hand in what they wrote, was no more at their own disposal, than the *Pen* is in the hand of an expert *Writer.*

" Hence, as far as their own *Personal* concernments, as Saints and Believers, did lie in them, they are said to make a *diligent inquiry* into, and investigation of, the things which the *Spirit of Christ that spake in themselves did signify,* 1 Pet. i. 10, 11. Without *this*, though their *Visions* were *express*, so that in them their *eyes* were said to *be open*, Numb. xxiv. 3, 4; yet they understood them not. Therefore, also, they *studied* the *Writings* and Prophecies of one another, *Dan.* ix. 2. Thus they attained a *saving* useful habitual knowledge of the Truths delivered by themselves and others, by the *Illumination* of the Holy Ghost through the *Study* of the Word, even as we, Psalm cxix. 104. But as to the *receiving* of the Word from God, as God *spake* in them, they obtained nothing by Study or Meditation, by inquiry or reading, *Amos*, vii. 15. Whether we consider the *matter* or *manner* of what they received and delivered, or their receiving and delivering of it, they were but as an instrument of *Music,* giving a sound according to the hand, intention, and skill of him that strikes it.

" This is variously expressed. Generally it is said the *word was* to this, or that prophet, which we have rendered, the *word came* unto them. *Ezek.* i. 3. It *came expressly.* It had a *subsistence* given unto it, or an effectual *in-being,* by the Spirit's *entering* into him, *verse* 14. Now this *coming* of the word unto them, had oftentimes such a *greatness* and expression of the majesty of God upon it, as it filled them with *dread* and reverence of him, *Hab.* iii. 16, and also greatly affected even their outward man, *Dan.* viii. 27. But this dread and terror (which Satan strove to imitate, in his filthy *Tripodes,*) was peculiar to the Old Testament, and belonged to the *pædagogie thereof;* Heb. xii. 18, 19, 20, 21. The Spirit, in the declaration of the *New* Testament, gave out his mind and will in a way of more *liberty* and glory, 2 *Cor.* 3. The *expressness* and immediacy of revelation was the same; but the *manner* of it related more to that glorious liberty in fellowship and communion with the Father, whereunto believers had then an access provided them by Jesus Christ. *Heb.* ix. 8. *ch.* x. 19, 20. *ch.* xii. 23, 24. So our Saviour tells his Apostles, Matt. x. 20, *You are not the speakers* of what you deliver, as other men are, the figment and imagination of whose hearts are the fountain of all that they speak; and he adds this reason, *The Spirit of the Father* (is) *he that speaketh in you.* Thus the word that came unto them, was a *book* which they took *in*, and gave *out* without any alteration of one tittle or syllable. *Ezek.* ii. 8, 9, 10, 11. *ch.* iii. 3. Revel. x. 9, 10, 11.

"Moreover, when the *word* was thus *come* to the prophets, and God had spoken in them, it was not in their power to *conceal* it, the hand of the Lord being strong upon them. They were not now only on a general account to utter the truth they were made acquainted withall, and to speak the things they had heard and seen, which was their common *preaching* work according to the *analogie* of what they had received, *Acts*, iv. 20; but also the very *individual* words that they had received were to be declared. When the word was *come* to them, it was as a *fire* within them, that must be delivered, or it would consume them, *Psal.* xxxix. 3; Jer. xx. 9; *Amos*, iii. 8. *chap.* vii. 15, 16. So *Jonah* found his attempt to *hide* the word that he had received, to be altogether vain."

Estius, in his commentary on the words, "*All Scripture is given by inspiration of God*," says, "It is rightly and most truly concluded from this place, that all the sacred and canonical Scripture is written by the dictate of the Holy Spirit, in such a manner certainly, that not only the sentiments, but also the particular words, and the order of the words, (*verba singula et verborum ordo*,) and all the arrangement, is from God speaking as by himself, for this is the meaning of the expression—that Scripture is divinely inspired." The theologians in the University of Douay, in which Estius taught theology, had made a decree of the above tenor, directly condemning Simon's opinion on the subject, and the Father Jesuits of Louvain. Here, then, is the decree of a whole University in support of the verbal inspiration of the Scriptures.

These Douay divines declared that they had examined the propositions of the Jesuits of Louvain, by order of the Archbishop of Cambray and of Malines, aud of the Bishop of Ghent.

" *The words of the Lord are pure words, as silver tried in a furnace of earth, purified seven times.*" Psalm, xii. 6. In reference to this passage, Bishop Jewell observes—" There is no sentence, no clause, no word, no syllable, no letter, but it is written for thy instruction; there is not one jot, but it is sealed and signed with the blood of the Lamb. Our imaginations are idle, our thoughts are vain; there is no idleness, no vanity in the Word of God."

The above extracts are not given in the way of authority; on such a subject no authority except that of the Scriptures is admissible. They are introduced in opposition to the assertions of those who speak as if the verbal inspiration of the Bible was a novel doctrine.

FINIS.

EDINBURGH:
PRINTED BY BALLANTYNE AND COMPANY,
PAUL'S WORK, CANONGATE.